FTCE

Florida Educational Leadership Exam Practice Questions

Mometrix
TEST PREPARATION

Dear Future Exam Success Story

First of all, **THANK YOU** for purchasing Mometrix study materials!

Second, congratulations! You are one of the few determined test-takers who are committed to doing whatever it takes to excel on your exam. **You have come to the right place.** We developed these practice tests with one goal in mind: to deliver you the best possible approximation of the questions you will see on test day.

Standardized testing is one of the biggest obstacles on your road to success, which only increases the importance of doing well in the high-pressure, high-stakes environment of test day. Your results on this test could have a significant impact on your future, and these practice tests will give you the repetitions you need to build your familiarity and confidence with the test content and format to help you achieve your full potential on test day.

Your success is our success

We would love to hear from you! If you would like to share the story of your exam success or if you have any questions or comments in regard to our products, please contact us at **800-673-8175** or **support@mometrix.com**.

Thanks again for your business and we wish you continued success!

Sincerely,
The Mometrix Test Preparation Team

Table of Contents

Practice Test #1

Leadership for Student Learning

Refer to the following for questions 1–2:

A school leader has been hired as the new principal of a public elementary school. State standardized test scores in English Language Arts (ELA) across all fourth-grade classes in this school have steadily declined over the past several years. Scores in reading, listening, and speaking have all declined. Scores in writing started out the lowest and have dropped the most since. The new principal and all fourth-grade teachers are meeting to study samples of student compositions and discuss how to improve writing achievement.

1. The teachers have each brought writing samples from their students to the meeting. The principal should advise them to take which of these steps first toward instructional improvements?

a. Use the samples to identify students needing remedial instruction.
b. Perform an analysis of all writing samples, and give scores to each.
c. Review all of the writing samples and identify and group student needs.
d. Identify samples for use as benchmark examples next school year.

2. Following the initial meeting, the new principal conducts observations of each fourth-grade teacher's classroom instruction. What should the principal mainly focus on in terms of improving students' state standardized ELA test scores?

a. Whether teachers are aligning lesson objectives with state grade-level ELA standards
b. Whether teachers are incorporating instructional strategies for diverse student needs
c. Whether teachers are implementing their lesson plans as written in classroom activities
d. Whether teachers are aligning lesson objectives with materials and teaching strategies

3. To assess and monitor progress toward school goals, which type(s) of assessment would be MOST effective for measuring student analytical and critical thinking and communication skills?

a. Performance assessments and journals
b. Standardized tests that measure achievement
c. Extended student group projects
d. Teacher's observations of students

4. Which of the following applies to both horizontal and vertical curriculum alignment?

a. Teaching the same content across all classrooms on the same grade levels
b. Teaching content aligned with state or district assessments and standards
c. Teaching to minimize achievement gaps through standardizing education
d. Teaching across successive grade levels including preparatory scaffolding

5. School leaders should regularly review and analyze teachers' learning objectives, assessments, progress, and achievement data collection and use their analyses to determine which of the following?

a. How well these elements align with one another within and across grade levels and curriculum
b. How well these elements align with state or national standards rather than with one another
c. How well these elements align with one another within grade levels rather than across levels
d. How well these elements align with one another across grade levels instead of the curriculum

6. Which of the following practices by school leaders most effectively improves teacher practice and student learning?

a. Reviewing student performance data and sharing aggregated results with teachers
b. Administering self-assessment surveys to teachers
c. Conducting regular classroom observations and providing timely feedback
d. Offering educational resources to teachers related to their identified areas of weakness

7. The dean of instruction conducted a classroom observation of a seventh-grade math teacher and noticed that the math teacher was not following the curriculum for the math department. When asked, the math teacher informed the dean that the students were not ready for the standards identified in the curriculum and that he chose to review standards from sixth- grade instead.

Which of the following would be the best response from the dean to the math teacher?

a. Commend the math teacher for addressing the gaps in student learning.
b. Require that the math teacher attend training on the math curriculum.
c. Model instruction of the standards outlined in the curriculum.
d. Direct the math teacher to teach the standards outlined in the curriculum.

8. Which of the following actions best demonstrates a middle school leader monitoring instructional practices and student progress to ensure that all students are prepared for a challenging curriculum?

a. Offering a summer bridge program for underperforming seventh-grade students entering eighth-grade.
b. Reviewing the performance of incoming sixth-grade students on standardized tests.
c. Evaluating the course grades of eighth-grade students enrolled in an Algebra I course for high school credit.
d. Comparing student performance on standardized tests to course grades to determine alignment of assessment.

9. The dean of instruction of a ninth-grade high school academy would like to monitor student progress for the grading period. Which of the following sources of data would best inform the dean of student progress?

a. Student portfolios of work samples from previous and current marking periods
b. Benchmark scores from the previous and current marking periods
c. Anecdotal teacher notes
d. Report card grades for the marking period

10. The math department is excited that for the third consecutive time, most of the seventh-grade students have earned perfect scores on their six-week report cards. The dean of instruction is concerned by this news and requests to examine student work samples and class grades. Which of the following is a likely reason that the dean is concerned?

a. The data may indicate that the students are not receiving rigorous curriculum and instruction.
b. The math department may have misinterpreted the student data.
c. The few students who did not receive perfect grades may be falling behind.
d. The students are likely committing acts of academic dishonesty.

11. A school leader requests that teachers identify exemplary student work in professional learning communities (PLCs) and post the student work in their classrooms. The school leader regularly visits classrooms to view and evaluate the work that is posted. Which of the following best explains why the school leader made this request?

a. The school leader desires to be involved in analyzing student work.
b. The school leader is encouraging teacher collaboration.
c. The school leader is enforcing adherence to the standards-based curriculum.
d. The school leader believes that all students should be recognized for their performance.

12. To gather feedback from key stakeholders about the relationship between their opinions on the significance of education and the school's vision and goals, which of these should a school leader do?

a. Develop a series of critical questions appropriate to this topic.
b. Develop a few open-ended questions to stimulate discussions.
c. Develop a school task force to interview all of the stakeholders.
d. Develop a series of meetings wherein stakeholders discuss this.

13. What is the most accurate definition of a learning objective?

a. What educators hope to accomplish during their instruction
b. What educators are supposed instruct the students
c. What students expect teachers to instruct them
d. What educators expect students to be able to do via instruction

14. As part of an overall school reform initiative, a principal plans to distribute leadership among educators and other stakeholders for implementing school goals. Which research findings exist to inform this decision?

a. Distributing leadership improves professional development but nothing else.
b. Educational reform changes demand efforts requiring a few superior leaders.
c. The capacity building needed for school improvement limits leader numbers.
d. School reform initiatives all share implicit distributed leadership in common.

15. Which of the following barriers would interfere the most with achieving a goal of increased student achievement in math?

a. A shortage of calculators
b. A lack of community support
c. The adoption of a new math textbook
d. The unexpected resignation of a math teacher

16. To create a culture of high expectations for students, some school leaders and teachers have instituted "no zeroes" grading policies wherein students received progressive interventions and new due dates to achieve at least 70% on assignments instead of 0% the first time. What best reflects student outcomes?

a. Far fewer students received F grades.
b. Missed assignments remained equal.
c. More students received a D grade.
d. More students received extra help.

17. How can attending district school board meetings most help a school leader who is new to a school and community in both informing the leader and promoting leader willingness to change positions or beliefs about educational issues?

a. By discovering how diverse the new school district is
b. By witnessing how school boards accentuate diversity
c. By seeing how school differences correlate to distance
d. By realizing how districts are managed just like schools

Refer to the following for questions 18–19:

An assistant principal analyzes student performance data for the grading period and notices that a class of students consistently performs well in reading and has not demonstrated growth. The assistant principal is growing increasingly concerned about the quality of learning on campus.

18. Which of the following would be the best source of data for the principal to examine next?

a. Student survey data
b. Teacher survey data
c. Classroom observation data
d. Class size and student to teacher ratios

19. A school principal has reviewed assessment data and is concerned about the quality of learning on campus. Which of the following would be the best source of data for the principal to examine next?

a. Student survey data
b. Teacher survey data
c. Classroom observation data
d. Class size and student to teacher ratios

20. Researchers for state education departments report that school leaders they surveyed found which of the following to be their most important role?

a. Creating a supportive environment for teaching and learning
b. Supporting parent involvement in the education of students
c. Managing the school budget and procuring additional funds
d. Ensuring and maintaining safety and discipline in the school

21. To build a positive culture of learning and high expectations, school leaders can guide teachers to identify instructional activities that are aligned to the curriculum and have been proven to be effective. Which of the following is an indicator of effective implementation of instructional activities?

a. Differentiated instruction
b. Increased student attendance
c. Flexible student grouping
d. Focused discussions and effective interaction between students

22. Which of the following would provide the most valid indication of a culture of high expectations?

a. Setting campus goals above minimum standards
b. Hosting award ceremonies for high-achieving students
c. Recognizing the Teacher of the Year publicly
d. Holding regular community meetings to discuss school performance with stakeholders

23. In many public-school districts, students with certain linguistic and/or cultural backgrounds are disproportionately enrolled in special education programs. How can a school leader best address this type of overrepresentation?

a. Examine current school procedures for assigning grade levels to students.
b. Examine instructional strategies targeting students referred to special education.
c. Examine instruments used to evaluate student need for special education.
d. Examine the curriculum and related expectations of student achievement.

24. Among standards informing effective professional development (PD) for teachers, which is/are most characteristic of strong school leaders?

a. Valuing ongoing learning, promoting continuous improvement, inquiry, collaboration, and problem-solving
b. Realizing good PD's value, promoting teacher participation, and communicating PD benefits to stakeholders
c. Human, financial, and temporal contributions; allocation coordination; and investment return assessments
d. Rigorous analysis of varied, disaggregated student data for proficiency standards, learning gaps, and results

25. Experts advise school leaders to create a clear vision for the best use of school-wide student achievement data and to communicate this vision. What else do they recommend for using these data?

a. School leaders should institute supports to develop a data-driven school culture.
b. School leaders should instruct faculty, not students, to understand and use data.
c. School leaders should develop and maintain data systems specific to the school.
d. School leaders should separate data from the cycle of continuous improvement.

26. A school leader wants to help develop staff leadership skills that are going to support the school vision. Which tasks would be appropriate to aid staff members in developing an increased diversity of knowledge about and skills related to school administration?

a. Serve on school leadership teams, lead faculty study groups, help on school improvement projects, and lead curriculum planning committees.
b. Help screen and interview job applicants, attend district meetings, work on less familiar projects, and help others work with challenging parents.
c. Discuss reasons and ways that school leaders handled situations as opportunities to observe and reflect, and journal leader practice observations.
d. Join and participate in professional organizations, mentor new employees, and present information to other members of the school staff.

27. Which of the following is a primary benefit of distributed leadership?

a. Distributed leadership helps to maintain status quo, especially in high-performing schools.
b. School leaders who practice distributive leadership are less stressed because they are able to delegate responsibilities.
c. Practicing distributive leadership builds capacity in others and develops followers into leaders.
d. Distributive leadership helps to identify weak team members that need to be replaced.

28. A principal forms and helps train a school vision oversight team before involving the whole faculty in developing a school vision statement. What best describes the primary purpose of this team?

a. To draft the vision because most school faculties are too big to be productively involved
b. To introduce the concept, engage faculty in writing a vision, and synthesize all their input
c. To represent the school leadership team on a smaller level by delegating some members
d. To represent all school department staff, including those who are not already educational leaders

29. A principal has assembled a school vision oversight team and provided them with a variety of school data for background knowledge. The team is ready to engage school staff in developing a new school vision. Faculty members review the current vision statement, examples of others' vision statements, and school data. The team divides staff into groups with discussion questions; for example, "What kind of school do we aspire to be?" What other question would apply?

a. "How is our school just the same as any other school?"
b. "What do we think our vision statement should reflect?"
c. "What should we keep on doing to realize this vision?"
d. "What is evidence we are meeting the current vision?"

30. Research into achievement gaps in suburban schools known for excellence found which of the following about students from racial and ethnic minority groups?

a. Black and Latino students spent less time on homework and completed homework less.
b. Researchers attributed differences in grades and homework to motivation and effort.
c. Asian students had higher grades and finished more homework by spending equal time.
d. Researchers attributed grade and homework differences to skill and home support gaps.

31. Which of the following actions best demonstrates that a principal makes decisions to improve instruction based on evidence from student data?

a. Meeting with parents frequently during grading periods
b. Conducting meetings for Professional Learning Committees based on grade levels and subject areas
c. Requiring teachers to host tutorial sessions for students after the regular school day
d. Submitting reports to district office personnel after each grading period

32. Which of the following is true regarding best practices for school leaders when giving teachers observational feedback?

a. Leaders should give feedback statements rather than asking questions.
b. Leaders should disregard strengths to focus on improving weaknesses.
c. Leaders should emphasize all identified areas for improvement equally.
d. Leaders should include some specific next steps attainable for teachers.

33. Which of the following should school principals primarily look for when observing teachers in classrooms for evaluation purposes?

a. They should focus on what students want to learn rather than what they want them to learn.
b. They should look for how comfortable the teacher is with the lesson content and method of delivery.
c. They should look for evidence of learning such as student responses to checks for understanding and student work products.
d. They should focus on physical classroom setup.

34. To evaluate teacher effectiveness in applying instructional strategies, school leaders need a working knowledge of student-centered, research-based teaching methods. What is most true about these?

a. The Socratic method is a useful, research-based strategy for delivering instruction.
b. Project-based learning requires technology integration in order to be implemented effectively.
c. Cooperative learning has been proven to be an effective, research-based instructional strategy.
d. It is necessary for teachers to utilize technology to deliver instruction in order to be effective.

35. According to multiple research studies, what is a characteristic of school leaders related to evaluating teacher effectiveness?

a. The most effective school leaders are better at identifying the best candidates for hiring as teachers.
b. The most effective school leaders are better at identifying the best and worst teachers on their staff.
c. The most effective teachers are attracted to the schools whose leaders have hired the best teachers.
d. The most effective school leaders are better at identifying excellent and average teachers than poorer ones.

36. A high school principal is concerned that ninth-grade students who read below grade level are not performing well on benchmark tests in reading and writing. Which of the following steps should the principal take to best address this concern?

a. Provide test preparation sessions for these students after school and on weekends and monitor student attendance to the sessions.
b. Integrate reading and writing skills into all subject areas and provide training to all teachers on fundamental reading strategies.
c. Increase the opportunities that students have to spend in the school library.
d. Purchase a reading software program that students can use at home.

Refer to the following for question 37:

The school principal reviews classroom observation and feedback with assistant principals weekly but often has very few classroom observations of their own conducted in preparation for the weekly meeting. This week, a teacher complained to the principal that the feedback from their most recent evaluation was not fair because it did not provide a well-rounded view of their performance.

37. What action should the school principal take to increase the frequency of classroom visits?

a. Make a commitment to visit classrooms every morning before the day gets too busy.
b. Clear their schedule on a specific day of the week to dedicate to classroom visits.
c. Plan out the classrooms that should be visited for the week and add them to the calendar with reminders.
d. Carry classroom observation forms at all times and visit classrooms when an opportunity presents itself.

38. What is the primary benefit of conducting teacher evaluations?

a. Evaluations can provide feedback to staff members so that they can grow professionally.
b. Evaluations are needed to determine who is not performing to expectations.
c. Evaluations can help identify the professional development and coaching that teachers need.
d. Evaluations can be used to remove an underperforming teacher from their position.

39. Which of the following actions best exemplifies a focus on school-wide rigorous curriculum and standards-based instruction?

a. Increase the number of advanced placement and dual credit courses offered on the master schedule.
b. Increase the number of students taking college entrance exams.
c. Evaluate campus-based assessments for alignment to the standards and curriculum and revise where appropriate.
d. Offer after-school tutorials for students who are falling behind.

40. Of the following, which is true about multiple assessments of student learning?

a. Different assessment types access different skills and learning styles.
b. Students must be re-tested often or they forget what they learned.
c. Summative assessments following instruction are typically sufficient.
d. Summative assessments enable adjusting instruction as it continues.

41. Which of the following is true regarding how teacher evaluation standards should be designed?

a. Teacher evaluations should reference clear instructional standards to prioritize student learning.
b. Teacher evaluations should be conducted by school leaders with a single standardized measure.
c. Teacher evaluations should be based on occasional observation and avoid critical commentaries.
d. Teacher evaluations should play a minor part in important decisions about teacher employment.

42. According to experts, which of the following is the most important factor in how school leaders evaluate their teachers?

a. Being motivated to evaluate teachers
b. Making time for regular observations
c. Making time for longer observations
d. Making evaluations discrete events

43. Which of these can school leaders appropriately do to prevent or eliminate racism and ensure cultural equality in their schools?

a. They can advocate for diverse representation on the school board and for equitable policies.
b. They should train their faculty in mediation and conflict resolution skills to settle disputes.
c. They cannot do anything about minority student overrepresentation in special education.
d. They can make official no-tolerance policies regarding racism that do not require consequences.

44. Which of the following activities would not be evidence that all students are being prepared for and have access to a challenging curriculum?

a. Students who were enrolled in pre-advanced placement courses in middle school are automatically enrolled in advanced placement courses in high school.
b. The school leader regularly monitors student performance data on tests and in classes to determine alignment of campus-based assessment to standardized assessment.
c. All students are administered college entrance exams on the school campus at no cost to the student.
d. Students who have a history of meeting satisfactory performance standards on standardized tests are offered enrichment courses to help them reach mastery performance levels.

45. The leadership team of an elementary school has implemented a new math software program for all students in grades three through five. After three months of using the program, the students participated in a district benchmark exam and they showed little to no growth in math performance overall. What step should the leadership team take next?

a. Abandon the program because it is not effective.
b. Develop a plan for monitoring the math program at shorter intervals to determine its efficacy.
c. Reduce the number of students using the math program.
d. Increase the amount of time that students use the program.

46. Which statement is true with respect to segregated educational services for individual student needs and integrated comprehensive educational services?

a. Students benefit more from specific educator expertise through segregated than integrated services.
b. A principle of service integration is student centeredness, that is, targeting the student as a failure source.
c. Educators should design their curriculum and instruction beginning with appropriate differentiation.
d. Educators should develop curriculum for average students and then adapt it for individual students.

47. How can a school leader evaluate and improve the school curriculum for cultural and racial equity?

a. Instruct teachers to view curriculum as pluralistic and unchanging.
b. Include multicultural education within the school curriculum goals.
c. Assure books include diversity but not look for prejudiced content.
d. Focus multicultural education on foods, festivals, and fun activities.

48. Which statement is MOST accurate concerning how school leaders can ensure that faculty instructional practices treat minority students equitably?

a. Leaders can best get teachers to model appreciation of diversity for students by talking about it.
b. If teaching practices conflict with student cultures, leaders instruct teachers to be aware of this.
c. Having all teachers know a few words or phrases in each student's L1 is simply token lip service.
d. Leaders should make sure that all staff members learn to pronounce students' names correctly.

49. Which of the following MOST accurately represents expert recommendations for school leaders to promote educational equity by influencing curriculum interpretation?

a. Allowing harassed students to establish support networks
b. Communicating with staff periodically about equity beliefs
c. Clarifying misconceptions about equity, like deficit theories
d. Talking about diversity issues regardless of staff discomfort

50. Researchers have identified which of the following practices that successful education leaders recommend to advocate for educational excellence and equity?

a. They develop equity skills that spread through the learning community.
b. They study system inequities to discover solutions to the problems.
c. They study equitable leadership to discover their parts in the problems.
d. They advise others to develop collaborative approaches across systems.

51. Which of the following informs how school leaders can incorporate diverse family and community aspirations and expectations into their educational decision-making and planning?

a. Family aspirations for children vary markedly by culture.
b. Ethnicity strongly influences family academic aspiration.
c. Income affects family expectations more than race does.
d. Studies find high family aspirations across demographics.

52. Which of the following strategies best addresses the achievement gap?

a. Disaggregating student data by subpopulations to identify disparities in performance
b. Providing targeted interventions to students who perform unsatisfactorily
c. Tracking student performance and making projections about future performance based on past performance
d. Exempting struggling students from meeting certain standards

53. School leaders need to access multiple information sources to understand and address diverse student and community dynamics. As one type of source, their state education departments can share leadership and accountability and support school leaders. Which example of this helps school leaders in their jobs by facilitating their analyses of school strengths, needs, progress, and trends?

a. Establishing online networks and electronic mailing lists for them
b. Strengthening resources and refining data collection methods
c. Organizing conferences designed especially for school leaders
d. Initiating mentoring and coaching programs for school leaders

54. To engage diverse family and community members, school leaders and staff must make efforts to bridge gaps in language, culture, literacy, education, and so on. Which strategy MOST addresses cultural differences?

a. Having multilingual staff interpret at meetings, trainings, school events, and home visits
b. Suggesting parents ask children about assignments rather than help with homework
c. Assigning parent and community rooms for teacher and other parent meetings and information
d. Hiring community liaisons to help staff understand parental beliefs about education

55. The Tripod Project and other research-based initiatives to close achievement gaps have identified aspects of student engagement. For example, when teachers help them consolidate new learning, students are prepared for the future. Among other aspects, which of the following opposing pairs described as leading to success or failure is incorrect?

a. Trust and interest versus mistrust and disinterest
b. Autonomy of students versus control by teachers
c. Ambition in learning versus. ambivalence toward it
d. Industry versus disengagement or discouragement

56. What best reflects research findings about factors influencing school achievement gaps?

a. School curriculum and resources correlate with student achievement more strongly than socioeconomic status (SES).
b. SES correlates more strongly with achievement than school resources.
c. Student SES correlates more strongly with student achievement than school curriculum does.
d. Student achievement correlates more strongly with SES and school resources than curriculum.

57. Which of the following is the least effective way that school leaders can create inclusive school communities?

a. Encourage students whose parents do not speak English to translate for them when interacting with school staff.
b. Provide video recordings and resources to parents who miss workshops and meetings.
c. Validate, honor, and thank family and community for supporting the school.
d. Hire parent liaisons to help parents access resources and services offered by the school.

58. School leaders and teachers are frequently frustrated about lack of family and community school involvement, particularly in diverse populations. Which is the most likely source of difficulty?

a. Educator attitudes are often unrealistic.
b. Educators attempt to use too many methods.
c. Educator efforts are often very intense.
d. Educator engagement is lacking.

59. Which of the following is true regarding how school leaders can foster equitable and inclusive educational practices?

a. The development of curriculum should solely be based on developmental appropriateness.
b. School leaders should model respect for diversity and offer multiple means for celebrating it.
c. Involving culturally diverse community stakeholders in school decisions is the responsibility of the school district.
d. Only school leaders are accountable to ensure equity for every student in all school programs.

60. Which of the following accurately represents how school leaders can promote equitable access to curriculum for all students and their parents?

a. They can make staff more comfortable in discussing diversity without promoting equity.
b. They can clarify school staff misconceptions related to deficit theories about minorities.
c. They can model equity in daily interactions, but should avoid confronting discrimination.
d. They can create safe environments, though student support networks are not their job.

Organizational Development

61. Which of the following factors may directly affect a school leader's ability to recruit and retain highly qualified teachers?

a. The number of recruitment fairs that a school leader attends
b. The percentage of experienced teachers already on campus
c. The school culture
d. The available technology on campus

62. Researchers have identified which essential findings about how school leaders recruit, assign, develop, and retain highly qualified teachers?

a. Effective schools avoid hiring good teachers from other schools.
b. Effective schools assign new teachers preferentially to students.
c. Effective schools improve teachers more but at the same speed.
d. Effective schools retain superior faculty more than other schools.

63. What has research by state education departments found about public perceptions of school leaders' roles?

a. The public believes school leaders most improve schools by requiring standardized tests for promotion.
b. The public believes school leaders most improve schools by recruiting and retaining superior teachers.
c. The public believes school leaders most improve schools by applying strategies to decrease class sizes.
d. The public believes school leaders most improve schools by getting more local control from the states.

64. How can a school and its leaders best control the quality of the teaching faculty?

a. Focus on retaining effective teachers to prevent having to recruit new teachers.
b. Focus on attracting, retaining, and developing effective teachers.
c. Focus on hiring and developing effective teachers rather than recruiting new teachers.
d. Focus on retaining quality teachers rather than firing ineffective teachers.

65. For the third subsequent year, a school leader has had 40 percent turnover of teaching staff. This high rate of turnover has impacted the campus negatively and the school leader wants to address this concern. In a stakeholder meeting, the leader asks members to brainstorm suggestions for addressing teacher retention. Which of the following suggestions should the school leader implement first?

a. Administer a survey to teachers to get their feedback on what they like and dislike about working at the campus.
b. Petition the district to raise teacher salaries.
c. Offer bonuses to teachers who produce good student performance results on standardized assessments.
d. Provide mentors to new teachers on campus.

66. Staff morale at ABC Elementary school is very low and is impacting staff and student performance. Which of the following steps should the principal take first to repair staff morale?

a. Host an all-staff pep rally to encourage everyone.
b. Create a committee to advise the principal on how to repair staff morale.
c. Buy gifts for the staff.
d. Administer a survey to identify the causes of low morale.

Refer to the following for question 67:

A new school principal administered a survey to school staff to assess the perceived culture of the school. The data from the survey showed that most of the staff felt that all ideas for the school came from the top and were forced down. The school principal wants to shift the culture and encourage staff to be innovative.

67. Which of the following strategies would best help the principal to meet this goal?

a. Create action committees made up of teachers and staff and give the committees time and resources to generate solutions to campus needs.
b. Place a suggestion box in the teachers' lounge and encourage teachers to submit their ideas for consideration.
c. Inform the staff that there are positions on the Shared Decision-Making Committee for teachers and that they would feel more represented if they engaged in the process.
d. Host a town hall meeting and allow participants to share their ideas publicly.

68. Surveyed school principals have reported that which of the following has been adversely affected since standards-based accountability systems were implemented?

a. Teacher morale
b. Curriculum and instruction
c. Student assessment practices
d. Expectations and achievement

Refer to the following for questions 69–70:

The school principal reviews classroom observation and feedback with assistant principals weekly but often has very few classroom observations of their own conducted in preparation for the weekly meeting. This week, a teacher complained to the principal that the feedback from their most recent evaluation was not fair because it did not provide a well-rounded view of their performance.

69. Which of the following is the best action that the principal can take to address this teacher's concern?

a. Conduct additional observations of the teacher at various days of the week, times of the day, and in varied circumstances.
b. Explain why the evaluation was accurate.
c. Find other staff members who can confirm what was written in the teacher's evaluation.
d. Show the teacher that all protocols and policies were followed in conducting the evaluation.

70. When increasing the frequency of classroom visits, which of the following should NOT be considered when the school principal observes teachers in their classrooms?

a. The quality and rigor of assignments given to students.
b. The implementation of strategies learned in professional development sessions.
c. Classroom environment and culture.
d. The teacher's tenure or contract status.

71. Which of the following statements is true about a school climate in which students feel supported?

a. Students find resources and support are readily available to them.
b. Students who share multiple classes are more likely to form relationships with one another.
c. Student roles and responsibilities are clearly defined in policy handbooks.
d. Student feelings of support are not affected by interactions with adults.

72. A dean of instruction of a middle school wants to increase the number and variety of resources that teachers have access to. Which of the following actions should the dean take to accomplish this goal?

a. Encourage teachers to purchase instructional resources and provide reimbursement for their expenses.
b. Survey teachers to identify which resources they would like to have and purchase resources from their suggestions.
c. Provide teachers with asynchronous, on-demand professional development sessions online.
d. Seek free and discounted resources from vendors in the local area.

73. To communicate information to prospective community partners about resources they have and those they need, which approach that school leaders have found effective for motivating community leader engagement is MOST based on evoking intellectually and emotionally meaningful connections?

a. Simply asking prospective partners to listen to what they say
b. Asking how education experiences shaped who they are now
c. Sharing the story of their school with the community leaders
d. Clearly identifying their school's assets and its greatest needs

74. Which of the following is an effective way to use community resources to support student learning?

a. Invite local churches to host a back-to-school drive to provide students with school supplies.
b. Partner with local businesses to provide free tutoring to students after school.
c. Partner with local businesses to host field trips for students.
d. Invite local businesspersons in the community to mentor students.

75. Which of the following is the most critical question to consider when using community resources in the classroom?

a. Are the resources aligned with the curriculum?
b. Are there enough resources for all students?
c. Are teachers familiar with these resources?
d. Are the resources expected to be returned?

76. A female member of a school's staff sends a letter to the principal. Her complaint is that her supervisor, who is male, calls her and other female employees by names such as "dear", "honey," and so on. The writer of the letter perceives this as disrespectful. In following up, the principal discovers the content of the complaint is confirmed as fact but also that the majority of the rest of the female staff do not perceive the male supervisor as disrespectful in his forms of address. Which action regarding the complaint would be most appropriate?

a. Telling the letter writer that other females on the school staff do not agree with her about the names.
b. Telling the supervisor that some staff are offended, and that referring to female employees in this manner is unprofessional.
c. Calling a meeting of female school staff and their supervisor to review laws on workplace sexual harassment.
d. Calling a meeting with the supervisor to reprimand him and ask him to make a public apology to staff.

77. Which of the following actions is NOT an example of a school leader functioning as an instrument of social justice?

a. Writing a letter to the State Board of Education regarding education funding
b. Participating in a community rally to protest the construction of a railroad through the neighborhood
c. Becoming a paid member of an education organization for urban school leaders
d. Campaigning in the school cafeteria for a political candidate in an upcoming election

78. A student reports to the principal that a teacher helped him with answers on the state standardized test. Which of the following should the principal do next?

a. Investigate to find out if the student is telling the truth.
b. Confront the teacher accused of cheating.
c. Document the complaint in case the school is audited.
d. Report the allegation to the district testing department.

79. During a classroom observation, a school leader notices that a student is sitting in the corner of the classroom and is not engaged in the lesson. The teacher does not attempt to engage the student during the lesson. When the school leader meets with the teacher about the observation and asks about the student, the teacher responds that there was no point in trying to get that student to participate because he was going to fail no matter what. The teacher's response demonstrates a disagreement with which educational philosophy?

a. Teach students to be life-long learners.
b. Education is the key to success.
c. All students can learn.
d. Educate the whole child.

80. Which statement is MOST accurate and complete regarding school leader skills for promoting staff collaboration in problem solving toward school improvement and reform to realize school vision and goals?

a. School leaders communicate school vision and goals to stakeholders, which suffices.
b. School leaders evaluate staff leadership abilities and select those with the best skills.
c. School leaders use consensus building and group-process skills in facilitating reform.
d. School leaders evaluate staff collaborative skills and select those with the best skills.

81. Which of the following is most used in self-assessment to facilitate professional development?

a. Teachers write in journals about their work
b. Teachers apply advice they receive to work
c. Teachers analyze videos of their instruction
d. Teachers benefit from others' experiences

82. Of the following, which accurately reflects a principle of adult learning that applies to professional development (PD) for teachers?

a. Adults learn best when participation in PD is required.
b. Adults learn best when learning materials are selected and provided.
c. Adults learn best when they are involved in planning the instruction.
d. Adults learn best when informed about how they will be assessed prior to participation.

83. Which of the following professional development activities would likely have the most impact on current teacher performance?

a. A self-paced book study program for all teachers
b. Online courses that teachers select and participate in at their own pace.
c. A four-hour in-person training conducted during the school year
d. A hybrid online and in-person six-week course that meets weekly for a cohort of teachers

84. Which of the following sources and types of data would be best to use to provide feedback to teachers so that they can improve student learning?

a. Classroom observations, student class grades, and summative assessment data
b. Formative assessment data, attendance data, and behavior data
c. Classroom observations, survey data, and diagnostic testing data
d. Formative assessment data, diagnostic testing data, and projected performance data

85. Which of the following actions taken by a principal best addresses the problem of having primarily novice teachers on staff?

a. Increased teacher observations and feedback
b. Facilitating collaborative and team teaching
c. Monitoring data closely
d. Providing tutorials for students after school

86. Which of the following is true regarding information and data that teachers should consider when planning for differentiated instruction?

a. Special population identification and past academic performance are the only data that teachers should consider when planning for differentiated instruction.
b. Formative assessment is not useful when planning for differentiated instruction.
c. Student interests should be a major determining factor when planning for differentiated instruction.
d. Student performance data, interests, and learning styles should all be considered when planning for differentiated instruction.

87. A high school principal has created instructional teams comprised of teachers from each core content area and fine arts. These teams plan instruction together and incorporate concepts from the various subjects in each of their classrooms. This strategy is an example of what type of instruction?

a. Differentiated instruction
b. Rigorous instruction
c. Cross-curricular instruction
d. Professional learning communities

88. Which of the following is the best example of summative assessment?

a. Standardized tests
b. Homework assignments
c. Practice assignments completed in class
d. Projects

89. Several teachers on campus have expressed concerns to the principal that there is too much focus on standardized assessment. The teachers suggest that they develop authentic assessments for student learning. Which of the following is the best example of authentic summative assessment?

a. Benchmark tests
b. Student choice of completing a project, essay, or performance
c. Oral exams
d. Allowing students to complete homework assignments at their own pace

90. Of the following, which correctly reflects characteristics of school professional development that will best meet student needs and achieve school goals?

a. It should be provided exclusively to professional teachers and faculty.
b. It should be separated from the job to enable greater perspective.
c. It should be differentiated to address individual areas of challenge.
d. It should be provided periodically but regularly by being scheduled.

91. What does research show about school leaders distributing leadership responsibilities for implementing a school vision and goals?

a. The most effective leaders are found to influence student achievement and school efficacy directly.
b. Today's schools cannot be led by one principal without significant participation by other educators.
c. The traditional model of single, formal leadership exists because teachers lack a principal's expertise.
d. Educational programs developed by one principal are easier for principals who follow to maintain.

92. As school leader responsibilities have increased, distributing leadership has become more important. Distributive leadership can have additive or holistic forms. Which of the following is correct regarding these forms?

a. In the additive form, collective work by all leaders adds up to more than the sum of its parts.
b. In the holistic form, every organizational member is a leader, regardless of his or her interactions.
c. In the additive form, all organizational leaders must "sink or swim" together, not separately.
d. In the holistic form, interdependent leadership among organization members is emphasized.

93. The school leader has established the school goals for the school year and is developing a plan for assessing and monitoring progress. Which of the following strategies would be most effective for monitoring goal progress?

a. Require leadership team members who have been delegated tasks to report on what they have accomplished each week.
b. Review student academic performance data in preparation for quarterly community meetings.
c. Establish time intervals for reviewing indicators of performance, such as monthly or according to grading periods.
d. Purchase and implement an electronic data management platform that sends automatic notifications when data does not meet predetermined thresholds.

94. The research literature about school principals' roles in realizing the school vision and goals, and aligning instruction with the vision and goals, affords which of these conclusions?

a. Principals with more effective schools focus on learning rather than on school improvement.
b. Principals with high-achieving schools have more confidence in teachers than in themselves.
c. Principals with effective schools delegate the roles of assuring instructional quality to others.
d. Principals with high-achieving schools communicate to all stakeholders that learning comes first.

95. A school leader has created a committee of staff members on campus that will serve as an advisory board for accomplishing the school vision. Members include the administrative team, school counselors, teacher leaders, and support staff. The most likely result of this action would be that:

a. The decision-making process will be slowed down because more people are involved.
b. Staff turnover will be reduced.
c. The leader will be viewed as a poor decision-maker.
d. Staff will be supportive of the vision and will help to accomplish their assigned roles.

96. Which of the following best describes shared leadership?

a. Authoritarian leadership
b. The delegation of authority and responsibility to other team members
c. Consulting others before making decisions
d. Publicly recognizing stakeholders that demonstrate leadership

97. Among guidelines for school leaders to embed standards-based professional development (PD) into teachers' jobs, which pair is described accurately?

a. Effective PD is student centered; teachers are actively involved in learning processes.
b. Job-embedded and school-based PD is on-site; teachers independently problem solve.
c. PD is supported and ongoing; teachers must know practical applications, not theories.
d. PD is part of district-supported systematic reform; it must cover new, unstudied trends.

98. Regarding strategies that principals can use to give teachers effective feedback, which is true?

a. Principals will make feedback fresher for teachers by delivering it unexpectedly.
b. Principals should give feedback unrelated to their expectations or teacher goals.
c. Principals enable perspective by delaying feedback after classroom observation.
d. Principals convey criticism best following strengths and by requesting solutions.

99. A school leader is looking to incorporate daily effort into professional development in a collaborative way across the campus. Which of the following professional development and learning opportunities is NOT collaborative in nature and useful for daily teacher activities?

a. Conducting action research
b. Professional learning communities (PLCs)
c. Daily reading of professional research in journal publications
d. Structured observations

100. When schools and leaders implement the continuous school improvement process, which should they do *first*?

a. Establish specific goals for school improvements
b. Reflect on instructional and leadership practices
c. Implement strategies for specific improvements
d. Conduct needs assessments for their schools

101. A principal notices that even though teachers actively participate in professional development throughout the school year, there seems to be little evidence of changes in instructional practices on campus. Which of the following questions best addresses the concern of the principal?

a. What is the process for giving feedback on the efficacy of professional development offered to teachers?
b. Are professional development sessions aligned to the curriculum, instruction, and programs of this campus?
c. How much does professional development impact the school budget?
d. How can I make time in my schedule to attend professional development sessions with the teachers?

102. Which kind of data best helps teachers to identify strengths and needs in their teaching practices, support capacity-building, and identify specific remedial student groups?

a. Formative data
b. Summative data
c. Student profiles
d. Enrollment data

103. Which of the following represents a principle informing school leader support and professional development (PD) of teachers throughout their careers?

a. PD must be continuing and supported by repetition and follow-up to change teaching over time.
b. PD for teachers should be focused on practice and not on theoretical bases.
c. PD is best administered as a stand-alone process within individual schools.
d. When school leaders furnish PD, they should be sure to include the newest, most popular topics.

104. Which of the following best describes what school leaders should consider when identifying professional development for staff?

a. Individual staff members' goals are most important.
b. School goals and vision always take precedence.
c. Individual staff member and school goals are of equal importance.
d. Professional development is primarily for accountability purposes and goals.

105. Which of the following is true about school leaders as role models for teachers in professional development (PD)?

a. School leaders should facilitate PD activities.
b. School leaders should participate in PD with teachers.
c. School leaders should monitor teacher implementation of learning from PD sessions.
d. School leaders should determine the PD offered to teachers.

106. When selecting professional development for staff, which of the following should a leader consider first?

a. The cost of the professional development
b. Whether the professional development has been effective on other campuses
c. The areas of deficit of staff based on observations and evaluations
d. The alignment of the professional development with the campus vision and goals

107. Which of these is a valid guideline for school leaders to support staff throughout their professional development (PD)?

a. To be job-embedded and school-based, PD must occur in the school building.
b. For effective PD, teachers must not learn passively, but be actively involved.
c. Because teachers are the ones involved in PD, it should be teacher-centered.
d. PD must be done independently to ensure individual learning and growth.

108. XYZ school district requires a minimum number of professional development hours to be completed by teachers employed in the district annually. A high school principal notices that each year, teachers have difficulty meeting this expectation and look for last minute professional development opportunities at the end of the school year. What action might the principal take to address this issue?

a. Personally deliver professional development sessions to staff monthly.
b. Allocate more money in the budget to professional development.
c. Monitor professional development activities more frequently throughout the school year.
d. Provide incentives to teachers who complete their professional development activities at the beginning of the school year.

109. The National Association of Secondary School Principals (NASSP) recommends that school leaders furnish comprehensive staff development in supporting student mental health. Which area of recommended training is most related to the Response to Intervention (RtI) model?

a. Early identification of students having or at risk of mental disorders
b. The use of referral mechanisms for school and community services
c. Strategies to apply in promoting school-wide positive environments
d. Models for consultation, coordination, and collaboration in schools

110. Which of the following describes a role of parents and other community members as it relates to educator professional development (PD)?

a. Holding educators accountable for results
b. Understanding which student learning needs are presenting difficulties for educators
c. Demanding and supporting quality PD that improves teaching, leadership, and achievement
d. Allotting time and facilitating PD that will help educators address student learning problems

111. To address inherent barriers like staff fear of the unknown and resistance to change, school principals benefit from knowing common kinds of inner dialogues employees experience around school vision development. What do school personnel typically ask themselves about this change process?

a. Not what is needed for the vision but if they will be able to live with and support it
b. If they believe they and the school can realize the vision rather than if they personally believe in it
c. Whether they will be able to continue their instructional practices, and why or why not
d. What the vision will expect and how their lives will change, as opposed to just practice continuity

112. A school leader is developing school goals for the campus for the new academic school year. Which of the following should be included in the goals to best support a culture of learning?

a. Increased student attendance rates
b. Improved teacher evaluation ratings
c. Decreased student dropout rate
d. Increased student completion of advanced placement courses

113. When developing a vision for the school, which of the following sources of information is most critical to consider?

a. School, local, state, and federal policies
b. Past school performance indicators
c. Feedback from students, staff, and other stakeholders
d. Performance of similar schools

114. A school leader unveiled the new school vision and goals for the academic year at a community meeting. Several parents and community members were not pleased with the presentation and were vocal in their opposition of the leader's plan. Which of the following was the most likely cause of poor community support for the school vision and goals?

a. The vision and goals were not aligned.
b. The goals were not rigorous enough to meet state and federal accountability standards.
c. Stakeholders were not included in the development of the vison and goals.
d. The community members do not support the school leader.

115. A school leader conducts a data review and realizes that the school will not meet an important milestone in the action plan for accomplishing one of the school goals. Which of the following actions should be taken first?

a. Begin developing a revised action plan.
b. Communicate goal progress with the appropriate stakeholders to identify the barriers and challenges that prevented the milestone from being met.
c. Identify who was responsible for the failure and offer corrective action.
d. Host a community meeting to share an update with all stakeholders.

116. Which of the following is the best evidence of clear and effective communication regarding the school vision and goals?

a. Stakeholders who understand the vision and goals can articulate them in their own words.
b. Stakeholders can memorize the school vision and goals.
c. Stakeholders offer suggestions for revision of the school vision and goals.
d. Stakeholders support the school vision and goals.

117. The dean of instruction is preparing to implement an online literacy program that the school district has just purchased. Which feature of the literacy program platform best aligns with the school's mission to use data to make instructional decisions?

a. The program assesses students' reading levels bi-weekly.
b. The program tracks students' growth over time and compares their actual growth to expected growth.
c. The program autogenerates reports of student engagement and sends them to parents.
d. The program provides all teachers and administrators with access to a data dashboard that includes all data collected through the program.

118. At the midway point of the school year, the school leader is surprised to find that the school is not on track to achieve the school goals for the year. What could the school leader have done to prevent being surprised by this information?

a. Established a plan for assessing and monitoring progress at regular intervals.
b. Delegated responsibilities to the leadership team.
c. Communicated the goals more effectively to stakeholders.
d. Created a committee to engage with the leader in the development of the goals.

119. To inform professional development methods, which of the following is the best format for adult learners, based on the principles of adult learning?

a. Formal
b. Directive
c. Hands-on
d. Theoretical

120. Which of the following strategies most accurately identifies the school leader's role in implementing professional development?

a. Staff development is the sole responsibility of the school leader.
b. A school leader should delegate the implementation of professional development to the administrative team.
c. A school leader should leverage teacher leaders in the implementation of professional development.
d. School leaders are directly responsible for implementing professional development but should utilize their administrative team and teacher leaders where appropriate.

Systems Leadership

121. During the annual summer meeting, the math department chair expresses concern that the math teachers do not have enough collaborative time to plan lessons and discuss student performance. Which of the following solutions would best address the department chair's concern?

a. Make adjustments to the master schedule to allot collaborative planning time for the math department.
b. Offer extra duty pay for math teachers to stay after school and plan together.
c. Purchase a technology platform that will allow the teachers to communicate asynchronously online.
d. Place substitute teachers in the math classrooms monthly to allow teachers time to plan together.

122. Which of the following best represents a threat to an emotionally safe campus environment?

a. Bullying
b. Crowded classrooms
c. High teacher turnover
d. High rates of student suspensions

123. Which of the following is an appropriate example of an action that school leaders can take to change negative school cultures and employee attitudes that interfere with realizing school visions?

a. Observe indicators of school culture among students and staff.
b. Design professional development sessions for teachers that address school culture.
c. Frequently recount successful accomplishments of goals related to school vision.
d. Hold annual ceremonies for celebrating successes.

124. School leaders and schools realize benefits from engaging community partners. Which of the following such benefits contribute(s) MOST to successful student interactions in the wider world beyond their immediate community?

a. Greater social capital through relationships
b. Access to necessary health and social services
c. Safe opportunities to experiment and lead
d. Adult guidance and positive role modeling

125. A school leader is approached by a journalist to contribute to a news segment about preparing students for an upcoming standardized test. Which of the following actions should the school leader take first?

a. Prepare a statement for the news segment.
b. Contact the school district media department.
c. Schedule a date for the interview.
d. Identify students who can also participate in the news segment.

126. Advanced technology integration in schools includes empowering students to engage in the learning process using technology. Which of the following best exemplifies students creating content using digital media?

a. Students access wiki pages to review lesson materials.
b. Students record themselves reading aloud for reading assessment.
c. Students design elaborate digital storybooks to prepare for a state writing exam.
d. Students create PowerPoint presentations about insects using photos from the Internet.

127. What have researchers found about the roles of school leaders relative to teacher risk taking?

a. Principals who follow traditional authoritarian approaches receive more respect from teachers.
b. When principals allow more freedom in curriculum design, teachers miss their leaders' control.
c. Teachers attribute their success to empowerment by principals who give freedom to take risks.
d. Researchers find that to meet student needs, school leaders must minimize teacher risk taking.

128. Which of the following statements is most accurate about how school leaders align school policies and practices with federal, state, district, and local school system policies?

a. State standardized assessment instruments are based solely on standards developed by states.
b. Individual schools directly apply state standards for developing their standardized assessments.
c. Schools directly reflect system standards, and yet ultimately are also aligned with federal policy.
d. Local school districts develop standardized assessments applying the federal standards directly.

129. Which of the following actions would be most effective for ensuring that shared vision and goals are implemented consistently?

a. Publishing regular updates regarding goal progress in the school newsletter and on the school website
b. Identifying barriers and challenges to vision implementation as quickly as possible and revising plans to address them
c. Delegating responsibility to others to assist with vision implementation, monitoring goal progress regularly, and holding all staff members accountable for fulfilling their roles in the implementation plan
d. Meeting regularly with internal and external stakeholders to solicit feedback and ideas regarding vision and goal implementation

130. Students of XYZ High School will each receive a laptop for school use at the beginning of the school year. The school dean is tasked with developing an acceptable use policy for students. What is the primary benefit of creating an acceptable use policy for students?

a. To encourage students to take care of the devices
b. To help students learn how to use technology to engage in instruction
c. To teach students how to conduct themselves online
d. To clearly communicate how the device should be used and the consequences for not abiding by the policy

131. The athletics director received notice that there will be random drug testing of all student athletes next week. The principal discovers that the athletics director acted against policy and advised all of the coaches to inform students of the upcoming drug test. Which of the following actions should the principal take next?

a. Give the athletics director a written reprimand for breaching policy.
b. Document the infraction in the athletics director's personnel file.
c. Inform the athletics department of the information breach.
d. Remove the athletics director from his or her position.

132. The US Department of Homeland Security has adopted the National Incident Management System (NIMS) for all federal, state, and local government agencies in emergency response. This system includes the Incident Command System (ICS). School district and building emergency response teams are organized based on ICS management functions. Which of these functions develops incident response objectives?

a. Planning
b. Logistics
c. Command
d. Operations

133. What is true about school leader responsibilities for documentation related to school safety?

a. They must communicate rather than document implementation monitoring feedback.
b. They must document their observations from monitoring safety plan implementation.
c. They must document school safety incidents but not related feedback to stakeholders.
d. They must not allow others to document the safety management procedures they adopt.

134. A constructivist model for evaluating educational programs incorporates multiple stakeholder perspectives. Which of the following correctly sequences the steps for school leaders and others to follow in this approach?

a. Discover stakeholder concerns, issues, and assertions; furnish a method and context for collecting and analyzing stakeholder feedback; identify stakeholders; establish a forum for negotiation; gather and disseminate information for negotiating; use an agenda for negotiations; reach consensus within and among stakeholder groups; review any unresolved matters; and make and deliver a report to stakeholders.
b. Identify stakeholders; discover stakeholder concerns, issues, and assertions; furnish a method and context for collecting and analyzing stakeholder feedback; reach consensus within and among stakeholder groups; use an agenda for negotiations; gather and disseminate information for negotiating; establish a forum for negotiation; make and deliver a report to stakeholders; and review any unresolved matters.
c. Establish a forum for negotiation; gather and disseminate information for negotiating; use an agenda for negotiations; reach consensus within and among stakeholder groups; discover stakeholder concerns, issues, and assertions; identify stakeholders; review any unresolved matters; make and deliver a report to stakeholders; and furnish a method and context for collecting and analyzing stakeholder feedback.
d. Furnish a method and context for collecting and analyzing stakeholder feedback; identify stakeholders; establish a forum for negotiation; discover stakeholder concerns, issues, and assertions; gather and disseminate information for negotiating; reach consensus within and among stakeholder groups; review any unresolved matters; make and deliver a report to stakeholders; and use an agenda for negotiations.

135. Studies have found that student achievement is increased most by school investments in which of the following?

a. Expanding teacher education
b. Expanding teacher experience
c. Increasing the teacher salaries
d. Decreasing the sizes of classes

136. In isolating factors that affect student learning, researchers have found which of these has the most impact?

a. Family involvement and support
b. Family socioeconomic status
c. Qualifications of teachers
d. The sizes of classes

137. What do experts recommend to school leaders for explaining policies to the school community?

a. Communication skills are less important than knowing and understanding policies.
b. Good communication skills take precedence over policy knowledge and understandings.
c. A speech to explain policies to parents is better than written letters.
d. School leaders should conduct a formal review of safety policies and procedures.

138. Which of the following is NOT true about the qualifications of teachers in public schools?

a. Teachers must be fully-certified to teach in a public school.
b. Teachers must be highly-qualified to teach in a public school.
c. A teacher who moves states may have to demonstrate subject-matter competency in the new state to teach.
d. Teachers in high-performing schools generally have more qualifications than teachers in other public schools.

139. In public school districts, which personnel are *not* likely to be directly supervised by the campus principal?

a. Bus drivers
b. Custodians
c. Volunteers
d. Cafeteria workers

140. Which of the following is correct about effective classroom management systems?

a. Tiered positive behavior support models provide both prevention and intervention.
b. Tiered positive behavior support models are only for preventing behavior problems.
c. Tiered positive behavior support models are designed to be behavior interventions.
d. Tiered positive behavior support models provide less time in academic engagement.

141. Which of the following strategies for implementing technology is most closely related to leadership in implementing a school improvement plan?

a. Utilizing technology as a tool to facilitate collaboration among staff
b. Utilizing technology as a tool to administer assessments to students
c. Utilizing technology as a tool for communication among stakeholders
d. Utilizing technology as a tool to collect, organize, and analyze data for school improvement and progress monitoring

142. Which of the following best describes the relationship between the school principal and the school board?

a. The school principal recommends the hiring and termination of teachers to the school board.
b. The school principal reports campus data to the school board at board meetings.
c. The school board elects or hires and supervises the superintendent, who in turns hires and supervises the school principal.
d. The school board implements state and local policies that the principal must abide by.

143. Challenges to school leaders for promoting student mental health include limited resources. Among such limitations, which is most related to federal accountability mandates?

a. Ratios of school counselors to students
b. School counselor responsibility change
c. Inadequate support staff development
d. Districts' mental health staff budgeting

144. Leadership is one of the factors identified by research as instrumental in implementing school-wide technology adoption. This includes multiple roles for school leaders. Which set of responsibilities is associated with the role of learning organization leader?

a. Making change a priority, supporting and encouraging teacher endeavors
b. Making sure that teachers have what they need to meet goals for change
c. Setting high learning and collaborative standards as conditions for change
d. Leading initiatives, resolving problems, and providing learning opportunities for faculty

145. A middle school is expecting a dramatic increase in the number of students requiring special education services for the upcoming school year. Which of the following should be the principal's primary concern?

a. How this group of students will impact current student performance data
b. The availability of human and fiscal resources needed to meet the needs of this group of students
c. Community resources for this group of students
d. The reason for the increase in the number of students requiring special education

146. The first year of a mentoring pilot program has been completed. The first year was free for the school, but the school will have to pay a fee if the mentoring program is to continue for subsequent years. Which of the following would best inform the principal's decision about whether to continue the program?

a. The number of students who participated in the program
b. Student feedback on the program
c. Community feedback on the program
d. Student performance indicators related to the campus goals

147. Which of the following categories represents the highest percentage of budgetary expenditures for public schools?

a. Student support services
b. Operations
c. Instruction and instruction related
d. Administration

148. The technology teacher informs the school leader that the computers in the computer lab are outdated and make it difficult to provide technology instruction to students. What action should the principal take first?

a. Ask the technology teacher to choose a computer model to purchase to replace the outdated computers.
b. Allocate money in the budget to purchase new computers for the computer lab.
c. Refer to the campus technology plan to identify the timeline for replacing computers in the lab.
d. Request a district technology support staff member to service the computers in the computer lab.

149. A middle school principal has been informed that there will be a cut in the school budget in the area of technology capital for the upcoming school year. Based on this information, which of the following represents the best action that the school principal could take?

a. Do not offer a technology class for students for the upcoming school year.
b. Assess the current technology on campus and determine how to use current assets for next school year's instruction.
c. Apply for local grants to compensate for the budget cut.
d. Ask the community for donations of technology equipment.

150. The fine arts teacher would like to construct a mural outside of the art building. The school leader believes it is a good idea, but does not have the funds to purchase the supplies required to complete the mural. What recommendation should the school leader make to the art teacher?

a. Host a fundraiser to obtain money to purchase supplies.
b. Ask the athletic director to use money from the athletics fund.
c. Charge art students an art fee to obtain money for the mural.
d. The art teacher cannot construct the mural this school year.

151. Which of the following represents the primary source of school funding in most states?

a. Allotments from the federal government
b. Grants
c. Donations
d. Property taxes

152. How can school leaders problem-solve and plan for best allocating monetary and material resources to realize school goals for students in economically challenging times?

a. By postponing school improvements to a future date
b. By making cuts in funds allocated to student services and programs
c. By ending programs identified as not helping student performance
d. By eliminating professional development opportunities

153. An elementary school conducted a pilot of a reading program over the summer and the principal must decide whether to purchase the program for implementation during the regular school year. Which of the following data points would best inform the principal's decision?

a. Feedback from the teachers who implemented the program during the summer
b. Feedback from the students who participated in the program during the summer
c. Student scores on assessments included in the reading program
d. Percentage of growth in reading performance from the beginning of the program until the conclusion of the program

154. The Federal Departments of Education and Justice collaborated to produce a package (2014) offering guidance for legal and fair disciplinary decisions, policies, and practices. What is most accurate about the intents of this guidance?

a. It aims to lower overrepresentation of minority students in expulsion and suspension rates.
b. It is meant to help schools establish positive learning environments, rather than focus on school safety.
c. It is primarily intended to reduce violent school incidents in response to rising rates of school violence.
d. It aims to make behavioral interventions federally legal rather than non-discriminatory.

155. A school leader surveys key stakeholders regarding the school vision and goals to learn what they believe about the purposes of education. Which set of stakeholder groups is the leader LEAST likely to survey about this particular topic?

a. Superintendent, central office administrators
b. Members of school board, parents of students
c. Community business owners, business workers
d. Students, teachers, paraprofessionals at school

156. The National Association of Secondary School Principals (NASSP) recommendations for ethical behaviors by school leaders include the following:

I. Fulfilling their professional duties honestly and with integrity
II. Obeying all the federal, state, and local laws and regulations
III. Basing all decisions on the value of student success and well-being
IV. Acting to change laws, policies, and regulations against education goals
V. Implementing the local board of education regulations and policies

Which combination of these could MOST present a conflict for a school leader in some instances?

a. I and III
b. II and IV
c. II, IV, and V
d. III, IV, and V

157. Under the National Education Association (NEA) Code of Ethics, Principle I, Commitment to the Student, educators are enjoined against doing a number of things, including that they: "[s]hall not disclose information about students obtained in the course of professional service unless disclosure serves a compelling professional purpose or is required by law." This reflects which of the following federal laws?

a. The Civil Rights Act of 1964
b. The Family Educational Rights and Privacy Act (FERPA) and/or the Individuals with Disabilities Act (IDEA)
c. Americans with Disabilities Act (ADA) Amendments Act Title II
d. Rehabilitation Act Section 504

158. On which of the following do the Individuals with Disabilities Education Act and the Family Education Rights and Privacy Act differ with respect to student records?

a. Requiring instruction and training of educators on records confidentiality
b. Defining which student records are considered to be educational records
c. Determining conditions for destroying educational records via state laws
d. Regulating records collection, maintenance, confidentiality, or disclosure

159. What is the MOST accurate description among ways that effective school leaders openly share data with students and staff?

a. Involving identified students for developing data systems
b. Involving designated staff in developing assessment plans
c. Involving students in knowing and tracking their own data
d. Involving overall school data as the basis for student goals

160. How can school leaders best promote openness and collaborative decisions in ethical school leadership and make ethical conversation integral to their school culture?

a. They can analyze the ethical implications of any decision for the school community.
b. They can maintain constancy in their ethical frameworks throughout their careers.
c. They can accept needed funding even if the donors require less effective methods.
d. They can regularly initiate discussions for self-examination and ethics development.

161. Regarding school leader involvement in lobbying to influence legislation that affects education, which of these is true?

a. School leaders must inform lawmakers regarding educational issues.
b. School leaders cannot lobby for their schools on any individual basis.
c. School leaders can only lobby through a professional organization.
d. School leaders must be professional lobbyists to influence legislators.

162. The National Education Association (NEA) Code of Ethics principle of Commitment to the Student prohibits which of the following actions?

a. Encouraging students to learn of various perspectives independently
b. Reasonable efforts to safeguard students against harmful conditions
c. Disclosing student information which is pertinent to student progress
d. Disclosing student information if not legally or professionally required

163. Which of these is true about the relationship between federal, state, and local laws, and local policies as it relates to the school leader's responsibilities?

a. The school leader must interpret federal and state laws to determine how these apply at the campus level.
b. The school leader is responsible for influencing policies and laws at all levels.
c. The school leader must adhere to local policies unless they directly conflict with state or federal law.
d. The school leader must vote for federal, state, and local laws in accordance with school district policy.

164. The majority of US state laws designate which school professionals as mandated reporters of child abuse and neglect?

a. Healthcare and mental health professionals, but not childcare providers
b. Teachers, principals, and other school personnel are required to report
c. Social workers instead of school social workers are mandated reporters
d. Law enforcement officers, but not medical examiners and coroners

165. The school principal was informed by school district personnel that a parent complaint had been filed against the school. A student's relative who did not have guardianship of the student called the school and was informed by the attendance clerk of the student's schedule and attendance. Which of the following best describes the error of the principal?

a. The principal failed to monitor the systems and procedures to protect the confidentiality of the student.
b. The principal had poor judgment in hiring the attendance clerk.
c. The principal should have taken the phone call themselves.
d. The principal did not make an error in this situation.

166. You are the principal of a 900-student middle school (6-8). The school recently formulated a school vision, which includes a critical goal of improving the academic and social-emotional preparedness of the school's eighth-graders for the transition to high school. Over the past several years, teachers and administrators in the local high school have become increasingly concerned about the level of preparedness of incoming ninth-grade students, who have been increasingly socially immature and lacking in vital academic and study skills. Various stakeholders (parents, students, teachers in both schools) attribute the problem to different reasons and would prescribe different remedies. You form a committee to improve the transition to high school for the eighth-graders in your school. Committee members include teachers, parents, student supports (social worker, school psychologist), a special education representative, and a curriculum coordinator.

Write a 150-300 word memo to the members of the committee about the plan to improve eighth-grade readiness for high school. Before you write the memo, state what assumptions you make about the school/community (rural/urban, demographics, socioeconomics). In the memo convey why you believe it is important for the school to succeed in this endeavor (improving preparedness for high school) and describe 2-3 significant aspects of the school's instructional program that the committee will address in developing its plan. For each of these specific aspects/factors describe a type of data or other information that the team should analyze and explain why this type of information may be useful in analyzing the specific area of concern.

Answer Key and Explanations for Test #1

Leadership for Student Learning

1. C: The principal should help teachers design and deliver instruction that addresses the standards on which the test is based. Identifying individual students with the greatest needs (A) would help them but not writing instruction overall across all fourth-grade classes. Choices (B) and (D) reflect steps in the process of improving instruction, but neither should be the first step. Grouping student needs is most related to declining group test scores, so identifying those needs (C) is the first step to improve instruction.

2. A: Although meeting diverse student needs (B), implementing lesson plans accurately (C), and coordinating learning objectives with instructional materials and strategies (D) are all research-based best practices, only aligning lesson objectives with state grade-level English language arts (ELA) standards (A) directly addresses improving students' scores on state standardized ELA tests, which are based on those standards.

3. A: Progress toward different goals often is best assessed or monitored using different types of assessment instruments. For example, performance assessments or journals are more appropriate to assess analytical and critical thinking and communication skills than standardized achievement tests (B), which are more appropriate for monitoring progress in academic competence. Student progress in working more thoughtfully through cooperative learning skills would be more appropriately monitored through extended group projects (C) or teacher observations of students (D).

4. C: Teaching the same content across all classrooms at the same grade levels (A), and teaching content aligned with state and/or district assessments and standards (B) are characteristics of horizontal curriculum alignment. Teaching content that progresses through grade levels, incorporating scaffolding to prepare students for the next grade (D), is characteristic of vertical alignment. Teaching to minimize achievement gaps through standardizing education (C) is accomplished through both horizontal and vertical curriculum alignment.

5. A: School leaders should use their analyses of these elements of teacher curriculum, instruction, and assessment implementation to determine how well they align with one another, within (C) and across (D) grade levels, across the curriculum (A), and with state and/or national standards (B) as well.

6. C: Providing ongoing feedback to teachers has the most significant impact on teacher performance. School leaders are responsible for evaluating teachers, providing feedback on evaluations, and assisting teachers with improving areas of weakness through coaching, mentoring, professional development, and other strategies.

7. D: School leaders must maintain rigorous standards-based instruction across the campus. If students are not able to meet the standards, additional supports and interventions must be offered to students to address educational gaps. The math teacher cannot choose to lower the expectations or standards for students without permission and documentation according to local and state policies. The teacher does not demonstrate a need for training related to implementation of the curriculum, but the teacher must be directed to abide by the curriculum as written.

8. D: Students must have rigorous instruction in the classroom to be prepared for challenging curriculum in the future. Students who perform well in class but perform poorly on standardized assessments are evidence of misalignment of course work to standardized assessments or inadequate levels of rigor in the classroom. Evaluating the grades of one grade level of students in a specific class is not evidence of ensuring all students are prepared for a challenging curriculum. Reviewing one assessment that was administered prior to enrollment in the school does not demonstrate ongoing monitoring.

9. A: Data must be compared from one point in time to another to determine progress. Benchmark tests are typically used to assess objectives taught during a certain period and do not necessarily assess the same objectives from test to test; therefore, benchmark scores would not necessarily compare the same data to determine progress. Student portfolios from multiple marking periods would provide an assessment of authentic student performance over time and would be most helpful in determining student progress.

10. A: All students receiving perfect scores for 18 consecutive weeks may be an indication that the students are not receiving rigorous curriculum and instruction. While there is an expectation for students to be successful in the classroom, there is low statistical likelihood that all students would perform perfectly over extended periods of time if they were receiving instruction at or above their level. Each student should receive a rigorous curriculum which means delivering instruction at an appropriate level of challenge in order to grow students academically.

11. A: Requesting that teachers identify student work and post it, then reviewing the posted work demonstrates that the school leader wants to be involved in analyzing student work. The posted work will provide the school leader with an assessment of student performance as well as what teachers consider to be exemplary work. This request does not directly encourage teacher collaboration as teachers could make autonomous decisions regarding their students' performance. Additionally, the request does not directly exemplify an assessment of alignment to standards. Finally, not all students are recognized, only students who performed in an exemplary manner.

12. A: To gather this kind of feedback, the school leader should develop specific questions that are critical in nature and appropriate to this topic. Open-ended questions will stimulate discussions of many other stakeholder issues and concerns (B). Interviewing them all (C) is impracticable or at best very time inefficient. Discussion meetings (D) are both less focused like (B) and less time effective, like (C).

13. D: Learning objectives are not what educators hope to accomplish, want to teach students, or what students expect teachers to impart to them. Instead, they are what educators expect their students to be able to do after they have instructed them in a content subject lesson, unit, or course. Experts observe that a common teacher error is to misinterpret learning objectives as things they plan to do during instruction instead of what they will expect students to do following instruction.

14. D: Researchers report a wide variety of school reform initiatives studied all commonly share one factor: leadership implicitly distributed among multiple individuals at schools. Studies also find that distributing leadership improves not only professional development of teachers (A) but also curriculum, assessment, and the development of professional communities in and among schools, led by teachers. Research finds the prodigious effort needed to make educational reform changes requires many good leaders, not just a few (B); broader-based capacity building requires distributing leadership more broadly, not limiting numbers of leaders (C).

15. D: Although each of these options could negatively impact the math performance goal, the loss of a math teacher directly impacts student learning and performance. Student performance in math is directly related to the quality of instruction that students receive in the classroom, meaning that the absence of a qualified math teacher for any length of time can be impactful. Additionally, the unexpected loss of a teacher can be a difficult obstacle to address in a timely manner. It is likely that losing a math teacher would negatively impact the goal.

16. A: At one school that instituted a "no zeroes" grading policy, outcomes included that 72% fewer students received F grades; missed assignments decreased significantly (B); 57% fewer students received grades of D (C); and 68% fewer students received extra help (D) because they did not need it.

17. A: By attending district school board meetings, a school leader new to a school and community can get a good idea of how diverse the school district and city or county; witness how school boards unite and organize diverse schools, giving them a common framework (B); see how schools can differ widely whether they are far apart or close together (C); and realize how managing an entire school district differs from managing a single school (D), promoting new insight and respect for school boards.

18. C: The school leader observing classroom instruction can also observe students in the learning process. Classroom observations can provide valuable information about instructional delivery, teacher quality, and student performance. Reviewing classroom observation data in conjunction with student academic performance data can provide the school leader with a more well-rounded understanding of the quality of learning on campus.

19. C: The school leader observing classroom instruction also provides opportunities to observe students in the learning process. Classroom observations can provide valuable information about instructional delivery, teacher quality, and student performance. Reviewing classroom observation data in conjunction with student academic performance data can provide the school leader with a more well-rounded understanding of the quality of learning on campus.

20. A: School leaders surveyed by state education department researchers believed that creating a supportive environment for teaching and learning was their most important role, superseding their roles of supporting parental involvement in education (B), managing school budgets and obtaining more funds (C), or maintaining school safety and discipline (D).

21. D: Focused discussions and effective interaction between students are indicators that the instructional activities are effective. Student discourse, whether teacher-facilitated or independent, is an indicator or learning and mastery of content. Increased student attendance is a positive student outcome but is not necessarily the direct result of a particular instructional activity. Differentiated instruction and flexible student grouping are instructional strategies, not outcomes.

22. A: In a culture of high expectations, staff and students strive towards high goals and excellence. A leader can create a culture of high expectations by setting campus goals above minimum standards. For example, if the expectation is that a school has at least a 90% attendance rate, the leader may set a goal of 95% for the school's attendance rate. Expecting students and staff to perform above minimum expectations creates a culture of high expectations.

23. C: Diverse students are frequently overrepresented in special education due to inadequate educator knowledge and/or preparation for distinguishing such differences vs. true disabilities affecting learning and performance. School leaders address this inequity best by analyzing assessment instruments used to evaluate students for special education—which often require accommodations, modifications, or replacement with alternative assessments for diverse learners—rather than grade-level placement procedures because these students need instruction enabling them to perform at grade level, special education teaching strategies, or special curriculum and expectations, all of which are after the fact.

24. B: Realizing the value of good PD, promoting teacher participation, and communicating PD benefits to key stakeholders (B) are characteristics of strong school leaders. Valuing ongoing learning and promoting continuous improvement, inquiry, collaboration, and problem solving (A) are characteristics of vibrant learning communities as professional development (PD) contexts. Human, financial, and temporal contributions, and assessments of allocation coordination and investment returns (C), are characteristics of sufficient resources and their effective use. Analyzing student data to identify proficiency standards, learning gaps, and assessment and behavioral results (D) is characteristic of rigorous data analysis by schools and districts.

25. A: Expert recommendations for school leaders in the best use of school-wide student achievement data include instituting supports for developing a data-driven school culture (A); instructing students to understand and use their own data (B) to set learning goals; developing and maintaining data systems on a district-wide basis (C); and incorporating data as an essential component of a cycle of continuous instructional improvement (D).

26. B: Of the options, choice B best describes activities that would put staff members into appropriate roles that would allow them to encounter new knowledge bases. Some of the other options listed include tasks that would be inappropriate to use as growing opportunities. For instance, choice A lists "lead curriculum planning committees," which would typically be reserved for a curriculum development specialist or potentially a department head. Secondly, choices C and D both involve activities that would not necessarily put the staff members into a position to learn new tasks, but only to ruminate on and practice information they already possess. The question asks for activities that would be particularly helpful for increasing the diversity of skill and knowledge bases, so the goal is to see a broader perspective on different aspects of the district and school. Participating in hiring screenings and interviews, attending district meetings, working on less-familiar projects, and helping other teachers with challenging parents all are likely to put a staff member into a place where they can glean new information about more aspects of the school.

27. C: Distributive leadership is a leadership style that shares leadership roles and responsibilities with others in a deliberate and systematic way. Providing team members with leadership opportunities builds capacity and helps to cultivate team members into leaders. Practicing distributive leadership also helps to foster change and improvement because the ideas and talent of team members are leveraged and utilized.

28. B: Although most school faculties are too big to develop a vision statement as productively and/or effectively as smaller groups, the vision oversight team does not replace or represent faculty. It is imperative to have all faculty's full investment regardless (A). The team's primary purpose is to introduce the vision concept to faculty, engage them in writing a vision, facilitate the process, and synthesize their diverse input (B). The principal may select team members from the school leadership team (C) or other staff representing all school departments, offering leadership opportunities to those not formally educational leaders already (D).

29. B: To engage them in developing a vision statement, questions the vision oversight team can ask small groups of staff (8 or fewer) to discuss include the following: how their school differs from other schools (A); what they think their vision statement should reflect (B); what they need to do differently to realize the new vision (C); and what evidence they can identify that they are meeting the current vision (D). These topics elicit key values, beliefs, and ideas as the genesis of strong visions.

30. D: Research found black and Latino students completed less homework, even though they spent similar amounts of time (A) as white and Asian students. Researchers attributed differences in grades and homework not to student motivation or effort (B) but to gaps in student skills and differences in home supports (D). Asian students had higher grades and finished more homework by spending more time (C) on studying and homework.

31. B: Professional Learning Committees (PLC) are designed to facilitate collaboration among teachers based on grade levels, subject area, or other commonalities. In PLCs, educators use quantitative and qualitative data to make decisions about students and are guided by the following questions: What do we want students to learn? What do we do if they do not learn it? What do we do if they learn it? Communicating with parents and submitting reports often include sharing of data, but do not necessarily indicate that the data is used to make decisions. Requiring teachers to host tutorial sessions for students is a beneficial intervention, but may not be a directive based on data.

32. D: School system guidelines recommend that, in giving teachers observational feedback, school leaders should focus feedback discussions by developing open-ended questions that target specific areas for each teacher, explicitly name two or three teacher strengths they observed, identify one area for improvement that will make the most impact on student learning and teacher development, and develop a few specific and attainable next steps for each teacher to take. Effective observational feedback should include strengths and weaknesses and recommendations for next steps should be clear and attainable.

33. C: School principals should look for evidence of learning when conducting a classroom observation. Students should be given opportunities to respond and demonstrate learning throughout the lesson so that the teacher and the observer can determine whether students are learning the content. These opportunities may occur as questioning strategies, discussion, or through guided and independent practice. It is important for teachers to be comfortable with the instructional content and method of delivery, but this is not a primary focus of a classroom observation as a novice teacher can be nervous yet still effective. Additionally, the physical classroom setup should be conducive to learning but is not the primary focus of a classroom observation.

34. C: Cooperative learning, the process of facilitating student collaboration, develops social skills, teamwork, individual and collective responsibility, and group interdependence. The Socratic method is useful for facilitating student engagement, assessing student learning, and fostering critical thinking, but is not useful for delivering instruction. Project-based learning is useful for active, hands-on learning experiences and does not require technology to be implemented effectively. Technology is a useful tool for delivering instruction, but is not required; technology is also effective when students utilize technology to engage in the learning process, making technology more student-centered.

35. B: Multiple research studies find that the most effective school leaders are better at identifying the teachers best and worst at increasing student performance among their existing faculty. However, researchers cannot determine whether the fact that effective school leaders also hire the best experienced teachers is more attributable to better leader ability in choosing teachers or to excellent teachers' attraction to schools with the best existing faculty quality. Researchers do observe that school leaders cannot differentiate quality among average teachers as well as they can differentiate better from poorer teachers due to lesser contrast.

36. B: Reading and writing skills are best taught and reinforced within the context of subject matter content. Creating a cross-curricular focus on reading and writing skills would best address the gap in performance among students who are not reading at grade level. Increasing opportunities for students to read is beneficial, but is less effective in closing opportunity gaps, especially when opportunities to engage in reading are voluntary such as after school or at home. Targeted test preparation has limited efficacy if attendance is voluntary and student performance is not monitored.

37. C: The best action that the principal can take to increase the frequency of classroom observations is to plan the observations into the schedule each week. This will force all other appointments and meetings to be scheduled around the classroom observations. Classroom visits should not be left to chance or they will likely not be conducted due to the many tasks that a principal may have to address throughout the day. Additionally, the principal should aim to visit classrooms on different days of the week and times of the day to obtain a well-rounded perspective of teaching and learning on campus.

38. A: The primary benefit of evaluating staff members is to provide an opportunity for leaders to identify areas of strength and weakness among the staff and to provide constructive feedback to staff members so that they can grow professionally. Leaders can use these evaluations to determine what additional support and resources need to be provided to support or improve the performance of staff members.

39. C: Evaluating and revising campus-based assessments to ensure alignment to standards demonstrates a commitment to school-wide rigorous instruction. Assessments should accurately measure the standards. Increasing the offering of advanced placement and dual credit courses supports rigorous curriculum for some students who qualify, but does not impact rigor school wide. Similarly, increasing participation in college entrance exams does not raise the rigor of instruction on campus, but encourages students to seek and prepare for college admittance.

40. A: Individual students have different learning styles, skills, strengths, and weaknesses, so it is important to administer multiple and varied assessments to assemble as comprehensive a picture as possible of each student's existing knowledge, new learning, and instructional needs. Multiple assessments are not used to keep students from forgetting. Summative assessments following instruction are not sufficient as they do not continuously assess student learning and progress, and they do not enable teachers to adjust ongoing instruction to be more effective as formative assessments made during instruction do.

41. A: According to the New Teacher Project (2011), design standards for effective teacher evaluation systems include evaluating teachers a minimum of once yearly, using multiple levels (4 or 5) for rating teachers, basing evaluations on clear instructional excellence standards prioritizing student learning, using multiple performance measures emphasizing teacher impact on student academic progress, making frequent observations and giving critical and/or constructive feedback, and making evaluation outcomes significant by using them as a major factor in important teacher employment decisions.

42. B: Experts believe that every school leader is motivated to conduct good teacher evaluations. However, they find one of the most important factors is whether school leaders make time to observe teachers regularly and frequently, even if only briefly each time. They emphasize that school leaders must evaluate teachers in a continuous process rather than a series of isolated events.

43. A: School leaders can change school board policies through persistent advocacy for equitable policies and a school board demographic that represents the community they serve. Both faculty and students should be trained in mediation and conflict resolutions skills for settling disputes (B). Regarding sensitive issues, such as cultural and racial inequality, every member of the community should have access to proper training on how to handle conflict. When minority students are overrepresented in special education, they can do something by administering culturally fair tests and revisiting eligibility determinations based on results (C). They should not only make official policies against tolerating racism but also clearly define consequences (D) for racist behaviors.

44. A: Student placement in courses should be based on relevant data. Automatically enrolling students in advanced placement courses without reviewing data could result in students being placed in classes that are too rigorous while students who were not previously enrolled could miss an opportunity to be placed in a challenging course. School leaders should monitor student performance data, ensure rigor and alignment of curriculum, and provide campus-wide opportunities for students when possible. To provide all students with preparation for and access to a challenging curriculum, students should have opportunities for an appropriate level of rigorous instruction based on their current academic performance.

45. B: Despite the students not showing growth on the district benchmark test, there is no evidence of the program's efficacy or inefficacy. First, the time period may be too short to determine if the program is effective. Secondly, it is unknown if the program was intended to have a direct impact on student performance measured by the benchmark exam. To determine the program's efficacy going forward, the leadership team must develop a plan for data collection and analysis at regular intervals. Only then can the leadership team determine the programs efficacy and whether the program should continue to be implemented on campus.

46. C: Researchers have found segregated services more likely to cause isolated skill development and fragmentation, whereas integrated comprehensive services require cross-disciplinary sharing of specific educator expertise, benefiting students (A) and colleagues alike. Although its staff design must be student based, a principle underlying integrated comprehensive services is that the source of student failure is the system, not the student (B). School leaders and other educators integrating services should design curriculum and instruction beginning with differentiation (C) rather than adapt it afterward (D).

47. B: To evaluate curriculum for cultural and racial equity and improve it as needed, school leaders can instruct teachers to view curriculum as pluralistic and constantly changing to meet changing student populations and needs (A); include multicultural education in the school's curriculum goals (B); not only make sure books contain diversity but also have teachers examine books for prejudiced or discriminatory content (C); and include multicultural education in books, other media, and learning experiences rather than focus it on only foods, festivals, and fun activities (D).

48. D: The best way to get teachers to model for students is for school leaders to model for teachers rather than only talking about it (A). If teaching practices conflict with student cultural beliefs, values, or practices, leaders must instruct teachers to replace or change these, not simply be aware of the conflict (B). Having all teachers know a few words or phrases in each student's first language (L1) makes classrooms welcoming, psychologically safe learning environments (C). Similarly, leaders should ensure all staff members learn to pronounce students' names correctly (D).

49. C: Experts recommend that school leaders establish support networks for harassed students as part of creating safe, welcoming school environments that make all students feel valued. School leaders have far more knowledge and means for creating such networks than students (A). Rather than talk with staff periodically, experts say school leaders should model equity beliefs for them through daily interactions (B). They should also clarify misconceptions related to equity, like deficit theories (C), and encourage staff to be comfortable discussing diversity issues (D), values, and social justice.

50. D: Researchers report that to advocate for excellence and equity in education, successful education leaders follow and recommend giving staff, colleagues, and other learning community members opportunities to develop equity skills. Developing their own equity skills will not automatically spread these through the learning community (A). Successful school leaders study system inequities to discover how they are part of the problems (B) and study equitable leadership characteristics to discover solutions to the problems (C). Additionally, they advise others to develop collaborative approaches across systems (D), enabling exploration of varying perspectives on leadership practices.

51. D: Studies find that, regardless of culture, ethnicity, income, or race, diverse families overall tend to have very similar high aspirations and expectations for their children, care about their success similarly, and (within their means) share similar active involvement in their children's educations.

52. B: Of the strategies listed, the strategy that best addresses the achievement gap is providing targeted interventions to students who perform unsatisfactorily. Disaggregating data helps to identify the achievement gap, but does not address it. Tracking and projecting student performance also has the potential to identify the achievement gap, but does not address it. Rather than lowering standards, holding high expectations and standards helps to reduce the achievement gap.

53. B: Improving the resources and methods available for collecting data is one way that state education departments can support school leaders in their jobs by facilitating their analyses of school strengths, needs, progress, trends, and so on. Another way state education departments can support school leaders in their jobs is by creating more learning opportunities for them (A), (C), (D).

54. D: Having multilingual staff interpret (A) addresses language differences. Suggesting parents ask children about assignments instead of helping with homework (B) addresses limited parental literacy and/or education by helping parents support children in nonliterate ways. Designating parent or community rooms where parents and other community members can meet with other parents and teachers and access information (C) addresses needs for linguistically, culturally, economically, and educationally diverse stakeholders; those with hectic schedules; and everybody else. Hiring community liaisons to help staff understand diverse parental beliefs about education (D), for example, that educators are authority figures they should never question, addresses cultural differences.

55. B: Student trust in the teacher and interest in the class lead to success versus mistrust and disinterest (A). Ambition in learning leads to success versus ambivalence toward learning (C). Industry in pursuing learning goals promotes student success versus disengagement from boredom or discouragement from difficulty (D). However, success is more likely through a balance of student autonomy and teacher control versus too much of either one (B).

56. A: Research conducted over recent decades finds that although socioeconomic status (SES) correlates strongly with student academic achievement, both available school resources and school curriculum correlate even more strongly with student achievement than SES. Researchers say these findings should motivate school leaders and schools to reduce achievement gaps rather than blame them on family or community SES.

57. A: School leaders should not ask students to serve as translators for their parents who do not speak English. Students may be unreliable translators and should not carry the responsibility of translating, especially in matters that the student may not need to be involved in. For parents who have missed school parent workshops, school leaders can record workshops for parents to watch later. They can create inclusive, welcoming, affirming climates by validating, honoring, and thanking family and community members for supporting the school as well as encouraging and maintaining their meaningful involvement. They can assign parent liaisons, which enable parents to access resources and services that the school offers to families.

58. A: Lack of family and community involvement is typically not a result of parents and others being uninterested in students' learning, working with educators, or influencing students' futures. It is more likely the result of unrealistic educator attitudes in expecting parents and others to seek involvement independently, and some educator methods are ineffective, like posting fliers at school when parents rarely visit, sending them home with students who forget to give them to parents, etc. Experts find educator efforts must be more intensive and organized to involve families and communities.

59. B: To foster equity and inclusion in education, school leaders should assure all their teachers develop curriculum and differentiated instruction that are *both* developmentally appropriate *and* culturally diverse; model respect for diversity in their own behaviors, and offer their schools and communities multiple ways for celebrating diversity; involve suitable culturally diverse community stakeholders in school decisions, which *is* their job; and hold all members of their school communities accountable for valuing diversity, equity, and inclusion, not just themselves.

60. B: School leaders can promote equitable access to curriculum for all students and parents by making staff more comfortable discussing diversity issues, social justice, and values, which will promote equity; clarifying staff misconceptions related to deficit theories about minorities and diverse groups; modeling equity beliefs and behaviors in daily interactions; confronting discrimination and stereotyping in actions and language; creating safe school environments where all students feel welcomed and valued; and establishing support networks for students harassed over cultural, sexual, and/or gender identity.

Organizational Development

61. C: The school culture can create a welcoming environment for new teachers, or it can repel them. When the school culture is positive, focused on students, and driven by excellence, teachers will want to be a part of that culture. They will be motivated by the positive culture and will recruit others to join the team. On the other hand, if the school culture is negative, then teachers and staff will likely have negative attitudes as well. Teachers will seek a way out of that school environment rather than encouraging others to join the team. This negative culture can negatively affect students' academic performance and behavior. If a potential teacher candidate observes a negative school culture, they may be unwilling to work at that campus.

62. D: Researchers have found that more effective schools can fill vacancies by recruiting and hiring more effective teachers from other schools (A); they assign new teachers among students using more equitable methods (B); teachers improve faster after hiring in more effective schools than in less effective schools (C); and more effective schools have greater ability to retain higher-quality teachers than less effective schools do (D).

63. B: Research by state education departments finds the public believes school leaders improve schools by recruiting and retaining better teachers more than by requiring standardized tests for grade promotion (A), applying strategies to decrease class sizes (C), or getting state education departments to give local schools more control (D). This shows public perceptions of the importance of the school leader's role in teacher qualification and professional development.

64. B: A school leader can best control the quality of the teaching faculty by developing strategies that address strategic hiring, development, and retention of effective teachers. Hiring effective teachers is important, therefore due diligence must be made to screen candidates and ensure that they have the appropriate skills needed for the classroom and are compatible with school culture. The school leader must provide the appropriate training and development for teachers so that all can grow professionally. Lastly, the school leader must be intentional about retaining effective teachers to reduce the need for hiring.

65. A: Each of the suggestions are viable options for the school leader to implement; however, the school leader needs to know why teachers leave or plan to leave in order to best address the problem. Seeking feedback from the teaching staff can help the school leader to focus resources on the most direct causes of teacher attrition. Once the causes are identified, the school leader can determine if the other suggestions are applicable.

66. D: The first step that a principal must take is to determine the causes of the low morale. Implementing solutions without understanding the causes may lead to wasted time and resources if the solutions do not address the perceived problems. The principal should collect data to identify the issues that staff may have on campus and then develop appropriate solutions.

67. A: Teachers and staff have more buy in when changes are made if they are part of the process. Creating a committee that does not include school leadership demonstrates the leader's willingness to give authority to the staff to promote change and a willingness to accept changes that are not generated by leadership. Suggestion boxes and town hall meetings allow staff to share ideas, but these ideas still must be vetted by the school leader as a gate keeper and may not fully address the school's current culture. Teacher engagement in the Shared Decision-Making Committee is vital for school success but will not likely address a campus-wide perception of top-down leadership.

68. A: According to some education experts (cf. WestEd.org), school principals and districts surveyed across the United States have reported generally positive impressions of standards-based accountability systems, saying these have improved curriculum and instruction, student assessment practices (C), and student expectations and achievement. However, many districts (over 40%) also reported that teacher morale had been adversely affected by accountability pressures.

69. A: Leaders should use as many opportunities as possible to observe staff performance in order to have a well-rounded view of their performance. The opportunities may include various days of the week, times of the day, and varied circumstances. A leader should be intentional and deliberate about seeking different opportunities to observe staff at a variety of times in a variety of circumstances in order to obtain a fair and holistic view of staff performance.

70. D: School principals should remain objective when observing teachers, regardless of their tenure or contract status. An evaluation rubric for teacher assessment should be used fairly and objectively for all teachers. A principal should observe what assignments the teacher gives the students, whether they are actively implementing new strategies, and the overall classroom environment and culture.

71. A: A supportive school climate occurs when students have resources readily available to them that can help them feel supported and to overcome challenges that they may face. The resources available should be based on student needs, such as counseling, mentorship, social activities, and others. A supportive school climate should foster peer relationships among peers intentionally rather than allowing them to happen by chance because students share common schedules. While policy handbooks for students are useful, they do not directly contribute to a supportive school environment. On the other hand, student interactions with adults on campus can directly impact students' feelings of being supported.

72. B: The dean should ask teachers what resources they would like and purchase as many of their suggestions as possible for all teachers. This would increase the number of resources available to teachers and offer them a variety of resources to choose from. Requiring teachers to purchase materials on their own is a disincentive if teachers cannot afford the upfront cost. Professional development is not a resource, it is training. Seeking free or discounted materials does not guarantee that the number and variety of resources will increase on campus if there are limited to no resources available in the local area.

73. B: Through experience, school leaders have found that simply asking prospective community partners to listen to what they have to say (A) can often communicate their school's needs. Some have found sharing the story of their school communicated what their schools needed (C). Clearly identifying their school's assets and greatest needs (D) helps school leaders and community partners both define their expectations. Asking community leaders how their own experiences with education influenced who they are now (B) motivates their engagement and assistance by enabling meaningful connections between personal experience and school partnership.

74. B: Community resources can be used in a variety of ways, such as providing school supplies for students, facilitating field trips, and providing mentorship. However, providing tutorial services to students most directly supports student learning. Tutoring students directly impacts student academic performance in class, whereas the other community resources support students' economic and psychosocial needs that may only impact learning indirectly.

75. A: Community resources used in the school must align with school programming. As a result, resources that will be used in the classroom must align with the curriculum. While it is important to consider a variety of other factors prior to incorporating community resources into the curriculum, it is imperative that the resources are aligned with the school vision and goals, which include the curriculum.

76. B: The majority of female staffs' perception of the supervisor's nicknames as inoffensive could indicate he does not consciously intend disrespect by using them and also suggests a positive relationship between staff and principal. Therefore, reprimanding the supervisor and asking for a public apology is not most appropriate. However, her complaint must be acknowledged and not discredited simply for lack of agreement. As the supervisor's address may not constitute sexual harassment and most staff members do not perceive it as such, a meeting to review laws is also not the best action. The principal should make the supervisor aware of how his habit is perceived by some and that he needs to cease referring to female employees in this manner. School leaders must also defer to policies and procedures outlined by their school board and district regarding sexual harassment, including policies on documentation and reporting.

77. D: A school leader cannot use their professional influence or position to solicit votes for a candidate on campus. Public school educators have a right to engage in the political process outside of school, but these activities cannot interfere with their job duties or cause a conflict of interest.

78. D: Testing procedures may vary, but there are specific guidelines for reporting testing violations. The principal should report the alleged testing violation to the appropriate authorities so that it can be handled according to proper procedure. Confronting the accused teacher or attempting to investigate the allegation could impair the investigation. Documenting the complaint may be a step that the principal will need to take after the allegation has been reported per protocol.

79. C: When a person finds value and worth in each student, they exemplify the educational philosophy that all students can learn. Some students may need more support or different resources, but they still have the capacity to learn. This teacher's statement that the student would fail anyway is in direct opposition to this philosophy.

80. C: Federal and state expectations of school principals typically include communicating not only the school vision and goals but also the school's continuing progress toward achieving the school goals to stakeholders (A); evaluating staff leadership abilities and developing and nurturing these (B); using consensus building and group process skills to support school reform efforts (C); and not only evaluating staff collaborative skills but also supporting staff needs in collaborative skills through professional development (D).

81. C: Analyzing videos of one's instructional practices is used in self-assessment and can also support reflection. Rather than relying on the observation feedback of a third party, the teacher can self-assess their proficiency in instructional delivery. Writing in a journal is used in reflection, not for self-assessment.

82. C: Adults learn in more productive ways when the choice to learn is voluntary, when they have choices among learning materials, when they are involved in planning the instruction they will be accessing, and when they are able to give instructors input about how their learning will be assessed.

83. D: Professional development sessions that take place over time, in contrast to single-session trainings, are more likely to have an impact on teacher performance. Additionally, when a cohort of teachers participates in a training, there is opportunity for collaboration and collective accountability. There are benefits of providing individualized professional development opportunities for teachers. However, when these self-paced trainings are not time bound or accompanied by accountability measures, they are less likely to have a direct impact on current teacher performance.

84. A: Classroom observations, student class grades, and summative assessment data would be the best sources of data to provide feedback to teachers to improve student learning. Data sources for improving teaching and learning should include instructional delivery (classroom observations) and student performance outcomes. Both formative and summative assessment data can be used to determine student mastery of objectives and efficacy of instructional delivery.

85. B: Novice teachers need increased support. Facilitating collaboration between teachers and encouraging team teaching provides support for teachers while simultaneously improving the quality of instruction delivered to students. Monitoring data, conducting observations, offering feedback, and providing tutorials to students are beneficial actions, but are reactive to deficits in instruction. The principal is being proactive by facilitating collaborative teaching so that students will receive good instruction in the classroom.

86. D: When planning for differentiated instruction, teachers should utilize as much data as possible that can be useful in determining how students can best learn. Identification in special populations such as special education, English as second language, gifted and talented, and others are helpful when planning differentiated instruction but are not the only factors to be considered. Student interests, learning styles, formative and summative data, and other relevant data should all be considered when planning differentiated instruction.

87. C: Cross-curricular instruction is the deliberate making of connections between various content areas so that students may apply their knowledge in more than one content area at a time. For example, students may examine the historical setting of a story in a reading class, utilize math strategies in a science class, or discuss geometric principles in an art class. Cross-curricular instruction is beneficial for students because it demonstrates the relevance of their content knowledge.

88. A: Summative assessment is assessment that is used to evaluate student learning for mastery. Summative assessment usually occurs at the end of an instructional unit or a designated period of time, such as a grading period or school year. These assessments are aligned to objectives or standards and are usually high stakes, which means they may count for a significant grade or may determine a student's progress in their educational career. A summative assessment may be a midterm or final exam, a research project, a unit test, or a standardized exam. The results of summative assessments may determine a student's grade promotion or earning of course credit. Results from summative assessments may also determine a school's performance according to accountability standards. Summative assessment results are often used by school leaders for instructional planning and goal setting for the subsequent school year.

89. B: Traditional methods of assessment usually involve a standardized test with closed questions that require students to select an answer from several choices. Authentic assessment allows students to demonstrate mastery of content and objectives in different ways within the context of the subject matter. This may include project assessments, writing assessments, and performance assessment. The goal of authentic assessment is to provide students with the opportunity to authentically demonstrate that they have mastered the content.

90. C: For school professional development to meet student needs and achieve school goals best, it should be provided to all staff, not only to teachers, specialists, and other faculty or professionals. It should also be embedded in the job rather than separated, differentiated to address the individual challenge areas of teachers and other staff members, and provided on an ongoing basis instead of a periodic one.

91. B: Researchers have found that the most effective school leaders have powerful influences over student achievement and school effectiveness; that these influences are indirect (A); that today's schools cannot be led by one principal without other educators participating significantly (B); that the traditional model of single formal leadership neglects utilizing the valuable expertise of teachers (C); and that it is harder to sustain programs and improvements instituted under one principal after that principal leaves the school (D).

92. D: The collective work of all leaders adds up to more than the sum of its parts (A) in the holistic form of distributed leadership, which emphasizes interdependent leadership (D). One way of describing holistic interdependence is that all members realize they must "sink or swim" together, not individually (C). With this in mind, (A) and (C) are wrong because they refer to the wrong form. Answer (B) is wrong in that in the holistic form, leaders are distinct, but work together.

93. C: When monitoring goal progress, it is important to examine data, not just identify whether tasks were completed. School leaders should establish regular intervals for reviewing the data related to the goals that have been set. For example, academic performance data may be reviewed according to grading periods whereas attendance data may be reviewed monthly. Electronic data management systems can be helpful; however, automatic notifications for not meeting thresholds may not be received in a timely manner nor indicate whether goal progress is being met or exceeded unless the school leader intentionally reviews the data at regular intervals.

94. D: Based on the research literature, experts draw these conclusions about school principals' roles in creating and realizing school visions and goals, including aligning instruction with them: Principals who focus on school improvement have more effective schools (A). Principals of high-achieving schools have equal confidence in themselves, their schools, and their teachers to meet school goals (B). To be effective, schools need principals who ensure instructional quality rather than delegating this role to others (C). Principals of high-achieving schools communicate to all stakeholders that the most important mission of the school is learning (D).

95. D: Different roles on campus can help accomplish the vision. The school leader can ensure the success of the school vision by engaging the internal community and including diverse perspectives in the implementation of the vision. This strategy increases buy in and utilizes staff members' roles to accomplish the vision. For example, the administrative team can lead projects and delegate tasks to others, school counselors can support the psychosocial needs of students to support their academic success, teacher leaders can lead and support the instructional staff, and support staff can support the logistics and communication of the plans.

96. B: A leader demonstrates shared leadership by assigning persons particular leadership responsibilities and granting them the authority to fulfill those leadership responsibilities. When sharing leadership, responsibilities are not dependent on job titles and can thus be delegated to any staff members who are capable of fulfilling the role. While sharing leadership can also involve including others in decision-making processes, shared leadership is best exemplified when a leader distributes power and authority to others.

97. A: Effective professional development (PD) is student centered, not teacher centered, and requires active teacher involvement in the learning process (A). Job-embedded, school-based PD can be outside the school if it emerges from and contributes to classroom practices and teachers perceive it as part of their daily work; it requires teachers to collaboratively problem solve (B). PD must be supported and ongoing; teachers must know and understand both underlying theories and their practical applications (C). PD must be part of district-supported, systematic reform, but school leaders should not let it cover new trends or fads that are unstudied, hence unsupported (D).

98. D: Teachers are more receptive to principal feedback that is not unexpected (A): principals should tell teachers their expectations and encourage teachers to establish goals before offering feedback related to these (B). As behaviorism has shown, effective feedback is immediate, not delayed (C). Effective feedback strategies include identifying teacher strengths first and then communicating criticisms in the form of requesting solutions (D).

99. C: Each of the options represents a supportive way of promoting professional development, but choice C is primarily an individual activity and not a way of building up a collaborative learning environment among professionals. Action research is the process of doing informal studies in the school environment to try to find improved practices. While the research is often done alone, the intent of action research is to share with other members of the learning community, making it a collaborative effort in most cases. Professional learning communities (PLCs) are teams of educators who work together to identify concerns and meet needs together and is an excellent way for teachers to improve their skills through professional collaboration. Structured observations are usually something the school administration takes on to ensure a quality control on teaching, but even though it often is top-down oriented, the process is inherently collaborative in that one professional comes and observes another teacher and provides specific feedback to help improve professional practices.

100. D: In a cycle of continuous school improvement driven by data that they collect and analyze, schools and leaders should first conduct a needs assessment for their school to identify where to focus improvement efforts. Once they have identified needs, they should set specific improvement goals. Then they should reflect on their teaching and leading practices for further informing improvement. This enables implementing improvement strategies. Another necessary step is to assess progress during and following implementation.

101. B: The principal should determine which professional development sessions that teachers are attending and whether those sessions are aligned to the curriculum, instruction, and programs on campus. The professional development sessions may be informative but may not be practically applicable to the campus if they are not aligned with campus goals. For example, if a teacher attends a professional development session on project-based learning, yet the campus does not implement nor support project-based learning, there will be little to no evidence of changes in instructional practice on campus as a result of attendance to that session.

102. A: Formative data helps teachers to assess their effectiveness during instruction (rather than after) and accordingly make adjustments to improve student outcomes. Summative data can assist teachers in identifying areas of improvement in their teaching practice but is often too late to identify specific remedial student groups. Student profiles from permanent records (e.g., demographics, assessment histories, family information, etc.) provide less detailed information to inform instruction. Enrollment data helps educators identify budgetary needs and student demographic distributions, but do not inform instruction, staff development, remedial student groups, or information plans.

103. A: To realize instructional change over time, professional development (PD) must be provided on an ongoing basis and reinforced through repetition and classroom follow-up activities. Teachers need theoretical understanding not only of the theory underling instructional practices, but also of how they can apply theory to practice. PD is best administered as a component of a comprehensive, systematic, district-supported educational reform process. When school leaders furnish PD, they should be careful to avoid topics lacking research support, unrelated to student learning, and popular new fads.

104. C: Staff growth though professional development is important. When identifying professional development for staff members, school leaders should consider school goals as well as individual goals of staff members. This will ensure that staff members are equipped to contribute to achieving school goals but also grow in areas that they have established personal goals.

105. B: Research finds that school leader participation in PD is what determines teacher and school-wide participation in PD. School leaders set an example for teachers by actively engaging in the PD that teachers are expected to engage in. School leaders should have a vision for PD offerings but can empower teachers to choose PD offerings that meet their needs. School leaders can facilitate PD activities but should also allow teacher leaders to facilitate PD as well. School leaders should monitor implementation of PD but this activity is not directly related to being a role model for teachers.

106. D: All of these factors are important to consider, but the leader must first ensure that the professional development will help staff meet the vision and goals that have already been established. A leader needs to be deliberate in selecting professional development for staff members so that the professional development is purposeful in helping staff achieve the campus goals and vision.

107. B: Although professional development (PD) must be job-embedded and school-based, it can occur even outside of the school building if teachers view it as part of their daily work duties and it emerges from and contributes to daily classroom practice. Teachers must be actively involved in the learning process for effective PD. It should be student-centered so that teachers learn to support student learning because PD is not for teachers' own sake. Collaborative teacher problem-solving is a PD guideline because it is valuable, addresses the issue of teacher isolation, and fosters professional and community respect.

108. C: The goal of professional development is to foster continuous improvement of teaching and learning. Professional development has limited applicability if it is all conducted at the beginning of the school year or at the end of the school year. The best action that the principal can take is to monitor professional development at regular intervals throughout the school year and to encourage teachers to take advantage of timely professional development that can impact their practice during the school year.

109. C: Whereas the National Association of Secondary School Principals (NASSP) recommends staff training in all these areas, strategies promoting school-wide positive environments are most related to Response to Intervention (RtI). RtI involves instituting school-wide positive learning and behavioral supports with three tiers of progressively more intensive intervention. Whereas the first tier includes universal screening, which relates to early identification (A), all three tiers benefit from school-wide positive supports, including students in Tiers 2 and 3, who receive additional interventions. Referrals (B) are only made for students not responding in Tier 3 and/or responding but needing additional services. Cooperative school models (D)are beneficial irrespective of using or not using RtI.

110. C: Parents and other community members must demand and support quality professional development (PD) that improves teaching, school leadership, and student achievement. School boards must hold educators accountable for results and provide policies clarifying that the purpose of PD is to enhance educator efficacy and thus student learning. Educators who organize and facilitate PD must understand which student learning needs they and their fellow educators have difficulty addressing. School system administrators must allot time and otherwise facilitate PD that will help educators address student learning problems.

111. C: Principals can help staff cope with changes by listening to and validating their thoughts through understanding common internal dialogues. These include wondering whether they will be able to live with and support the vision and also what is needed (A); whether they believe in their and the school's ability to realize it and also in the vision itself (B); whether they will be able to continue long-practiced traditions and why or why not (C); and what the vision will expect of them, how their life will change, and whether they will be able to maintain continuity in instructional practices (D).

112. D: The question tests the school leader's understanding of goals directly related to a culture of learning in contrast with other aspects of school performance. Participation in and completion of advanced placement courses is directly related to student learning and reflects high expectations for student academic performance.

113. A: All the information sources are valid and useful, but a school leader must ensure that the vison and goals of the school align with school, local, state, and federal policies first. After that alignment is confirmed, other information sources can be considered to develop the school's vision and goals.

114. C: It is important to involve stakeholders in the development of the school vision to help incorporate their varied perspectives into the vision and to increase buy in for the vision. Without buy in, community members and stakeholders may oppose the school vision and withdraw their support and resources for the school and school leadership.

115. B: Goal progress should be communicated effectively and in a timely manner, especially to those who are instrumental in achieving the goal. The school leader should communicate progress toward a goal, whether positive or negative. When there is regression in progress or a lack of progress, two-way communication should occur with appropriate stakeholders to determine what unexpected barriers and challenges to accomplishing the goal need to be addressed. Communicating regression in progress toward a goal is necessary so that corrections can be made.

116. A: When a school leader has clearly and effectively communicated the school vision and goals, others will be able to describe them in their own words. They will be able to communicate the vision and goals to others and explain the rationale behind them. Stakeholders who understand the vision and goals will propose ideas and actions that are aligned to the vision and will understand how they can participate in or contribute to achieving the vision.

117. D: The online literacy program collects valuable data, but the data must be accessible by instructional decision makers for them to be able to make data-driven instructional decisions. Collecting data without being able to access it is not effective for data-driven decision making. In order for data to be useful, it must be easily accessible by those who need it in a timely manner. In this scenario, teachers and administrators would be able to access all the data in one location, which would facilitate using that data to make decisions using that data.

118. A: A school leader must develop a plan for assessing and monitoring progress toward established goals. When monitoring is done consistently, the school leader will be aware of whether the school is meeting, exceeding, or falling short of established goals in a timely manner. Regularly monitoring progress toward goals will allow the school leader opportunity to make corrections in the strategies and implement actions, if needed.

119. C: According to principles of adult learning, adults learn best in more informal formats rather than how children learn by following a formal curriculum. They prefer guidance and choices rather than directive instruction. Both children and adults learn by doing, but active, hands-on participation is even more important for adult learning. Adults want to learn practical information they need and can use immediately in their work rather than theoretical concepts.

120. D: The ultimate responsibility of developing and implementing professional development for teachers and staff belongs to the school leader. However, a school leader should leverage the knowledge and expertise of the administrative team and teacher leaders in this process. The school leader may provide the overall vision and goals and delegate some of the responsibilities relating to professional development to others while holding all parties accountable for meeting goals and aligning to the vision.

Systems Leadership

121. A: A school leader must create structures in the school programming that promote collaboration for teachers. Allotting time in the master schedule for co-planning ensures that teachers will have dedicated time to collaborate, such as by participating in professional learning communities. Offering to pay teachers to stay after school may not be effective because some teachers may opt-out. Additionally, these planning sessions could interfere with other school activities these teachers may be involved in, such as coaching or tutoring. Providing asynchronous collaboration online could potentially be helpful, but it is not the best choice since it likely will not lead to real-time collaboration. Removing qualified teachers for planning can negatively impact student performance and should be used sparingly, if at all.

122. A: An emotionally safe environment is an environment where everyone can learn. It is free from all obstacles, negative emotions, and conflicts due to preventative strategies and quick resolutions. When an environment is not emotionally safe, children can feel fear, anxiety, and a host of other negative emotions. In an emotionally safe environment, both adults and children feel comfortable participating in the learning environment and interacting with one another. There is an absence of peer-to-peer conflict, peer-to-adult conflict, and bullying.

123. C: School leaders should frequently highlight successes related to accomplishing the school vision to show stakeholders that the vision is viable and successful. Ceremonies for celebrating successes and other ways of highlighting successes are beneficial but must be conducted frequently in order to change a negative school culture. Providing professional development for teachers related to culture can be beneficial but would not address issues with culture for all employees on campus. Additionally, it is important for leaders to make observations about school culture, but observations without action will not positively impact school culture.

124. A: Community partners can establish relationships that afford students greater social capital, which empowers their successful interactions beyond the community. Community partners also can expedite student and family access to services (B), which meet their physical, mental, and social needs more than contributing to global competency; give students safe contexts for experimentation and leadership (C); and offer adult guidance and positive role models (D), contributing to overall physical, intellectual, emotional, and social development and academic and nonacademic skills more than to specific, real-world, interactional success.

125. B: There are times when the school leader will need to effectively communicate with the media for both positive and negative reasons. The school leader should first follow the protocols and procedures outlined by the school district when communicating with the media, especially in situations in which the media attention is negative for the school or district. Some school districts centralize media communication and do not permit school leaders or other staff to communicate with the media without express approval.

126. C: Students designing digital storybooks is the best example of creating content using digital media. It is beneficial for students to access information using technology, such as visiting wiki pages. Students can also curate content that already exists, such as gathering photos from the web. However, creating content using digital media empowers students to use technology at the highest level of Bloom's taxonomy.

127. C: Educational researchers have found that principals taking traditional authoritarian roles are not respected by teachers (A); teachers resent authoritarian principals' control as manipulative, leading to teacher job dissatisfaction, but appreciate more freedom in curriculum design (B) and other work areas; and teachers attribute their classroom success to empowerment by principals who give them freedom to take appropriate risks (C), which school leaders must encourage to meet student needs (D).

128. C: All levels, from individual schools to state education departments, must ultimately align with federal policy to make major educational goals match the national vision. However, within this hierarchy, specific expressions of policy, e.g., standardized test instruments, reflect the next higher level. Thus, state standardized tests reflect federal standards, not just state standards; individual schools *directly* apply standards from their school systems, not state standards, which in turn reflect the standards of their school districts, which in turn *directly* apply state standards, not federal standards.

129. C: Shared leadership, regular monitoring of progress, and accountability of everyone participating in implementation are key elements to consistent goal implementation. Sharing leadership creates buy in for the vision and empowers others to take action so that the leader is not solely responsible for making progress toward the vision. Regular monitoring of goal progress using milestones and timelines keeps everyone on pace for implementing the goals and vision. The leader must also hold people accountable because each person must do their part in order for the plan to be implemented successfully and according to schedule.

130. D: An acceptable use policy is a document that dictates how students use the school's physical technology device, hardware, software, and Internet and network access. An acceptable use policy is a document that is usually signed to indicate that the user acknowledges the terms of technology use and understands the consequences of not abiding by those terms.

131. A: The athletic director acted inappropriately by breaching confidential information. As a result, the drug testing plan will need to be revised and some level of disciplinary procedures should take place. This breach of information should be handled officially and documented in the event that more issues arise later on. The infraction is not a personal matter, but is one dealing with breach of policy, so this should be made into an official written reprimand (choice A), rather than as a note in a personnel file (choice B). Finally, assuming this is the first major offense by the athletic director, the offense is not likely to be so consequential that the athletic director should be removed from his or her position as in choice D.

132. D: The Incident Command System (ICS) planning (A) function collects and evaluates data, identifies issues, develops action plans, and recommends future actions. The logistics (B) function identifies services and resources needed to support incident response needs. The command (C) function is responsible for overall incident management, public safety, information, and community agency liaisons. The operations (D) function develops objectives, organizes resources, and directs resources and actions to incident response. (The other ICS function is finance.)

133. B: School leaders must not only communicate feedback from monitoring safety plan implementation to school staff and students; they must also document this feedback (A). They must document their observations from monitoring safety plan implementation (B). They must document not only school incidents disrupting safety but also related feedback they give to stakeholders (C). School leaders are responsible for documenting safety management procedures they adopt, but they may designate others to document these (D).

134. B: Using a constructivist model to incorporate multiple stakeholder perspectives, school leaders first identify who stakeholders are to then discover their concerns; supply a method and frame of reference for obtaining and analyzing stakeholders' input; and bring stakeholder groups to consensus. If consensus building hits an impasse, leaders should have an agenda for negotiations; procure and disseminate information for negotiating with disagreeing stakeholders; and establish a forum for negotiations. Once negotiations are concluded, school leaders make and deliver a report to the stakeholders and then review any unresolved stakeholder issues.

135. A: Studies comparing school investments have found that investing in expanding teacher education (A) increases student achievement more than expanding teacher experience (B), increasing teacher salaries (C), or decreasing class size (D). This is significant considering how many critics have blamed lack of student achievement on new or inexperienced teachers, inadequate teacher payment, and excessive class sizes more than on lack of teacher professional development.

136. C: Researchers have found that among family involvement and support (A), family socioeconomic status (B), qualifications of teachers (C), and the sizes of classes (D), 44% of the impact on student learning is attributed to teacher qualifications. This means that the other 56% of the impact is divided among the other three factors; so of these four factors, teacher qualifications have the most impact on student learning.

137. D: School leaders must combine enough knowledge and understanding of policies to follow and administer them (A) with good enough communication skills to explain them to the school community (B). Regarding school safety policies and procedures in particular, experts from the National Association of School Psychologists (NASP) recommend school leaders write letters to parents for their reference. Parents cannot remember or review this information from speeches (C). NASP also recommends school leaders conduct formal reviews of safety policies and procedures (D) to assure they address all potential issues.

138. A: In some states, teachers do not have to be fully certified to teach in a public school. Teachers who are new to the profession and may be enrolled in an alternative teacher certification program may be allowed to teach in a public school on a probationary status. However, all teachers must demonstrate subject-matter competency prior to being deemed highly qualified and able to teach in a public school. States may vary in their requirements for teacher certification; therefore, a teacher who is highly qualified in one state may have to meet additional qualifications if they move to another state.

139. A: Traditionally, bus drivers are considered school support staff, typically under the district Transportation Department. They serve multiple school locations and are usually supervised by an employee in the Transportation Department. Custodians and cafeteria workers are often dedicated to one campus and may be supervised by the campus principal. Volunteers are unpaid and not officially school district employees, but are supervised by the campus principal to ensure compliance with policies and procedures. However, school districts may have differing organizational polices and supervision of campus personnel.

140. A: Tiered positive behavior support models have been found highly effective as school-wide classroom management systems because they incorporate not only prevention of behavior problems before they occur, but also interventions for existing or developing behavior problems. Also, by reducing the incidence of problem behaviors, these models provide *more* time for students to be engaged academically.

141. D: A primary aspect of implementing a school improvement plan is to use data to assess goal progress and completion. Integrating technology tools to accomplish this can improve the ease at which school improvement progress can be measured and improve the timeliness and accuracy of response to progress checks. Utilizing technology in other areas such as to facilitate collaboration, administer assessments, and communicate with stakeholders are valuable; however, utilizing technology to collect, organize, and analyze data for school improvement and progress monitoring is most closely related to the implementation of the school improvement plan.

142. C: The school board elects or hires and supervises the superintendent, who in turns hires and supervises the school principal. In the hierarchy of public education leadership, the school board makes policy decisions based on state and local legislature and the superintendent implements these policies. School principals apply these policies to the daily operations of the school. There may be instances in which a principal participates in a school board meeting, such as by reporting data or speaking, but these activities are not part of the regular responsibilities of a principal in relation to the school board.

143. B: Among resource limitations, inadequate school counselor-to-student ratios are attributable to funding and budget cuts, not accountability mandates. Inadequate in-service development for new support staff is attributable to various factors, including cultural influences stigmatizing mental health issues, lowering their priority in schools; leadership and organizational deficits; and funding deficits, ineffective resource allocation, etc.—not accountability mandates. Inadequate school district mental health budgeting is not federally mandated for accountability. Federal accountability requirements have changed school counselor responsibilities from addressing student mental health to addressing student academic achievement, reducing professional support services.

144. C: Among school principals' roles in leading the implementation of school-wide technology adoption, prioritizing change and supporting and encouraging faculty (A) are responsibilities associated with the role of motivator and cheerleader. Assuring teachers have what they need to meet change goals (B) is associated with the role of resource provider. Establishing conditions for change by setting standards for learning and collaboration (C) is associated with the role of learning organization leader. Leading change initiatives, resolving problems, and providing learning opportunities for faculty (D) are associated with the role of facilitator.

145. B: Although the principal should be concerned with a variety of ways that this influx of students may impact the current instructional program, the primary concern should be how equipped the school is to provide this special population of students with an appropriate education. Human resources may include teachers and paraprofessionals. Fiscal resources may include furniture, equipment, technology, and other physical resources needed to support instruction.

146. D: Although the other sources of information can be helpful, the principal must ensure that all funds allotted in the school budget are aligned with the campus vision and goals. When school funds are utilized, there must be a return on the investment that aligns with the vision and goals for the school. Programs and resources that do not align with the school vision and goals must be deprioritized or even eliminated.

147. C: Most school expenditures are related to classroom instruction. These expenditures include teacher salaries, libraries, professional development for teachers, curriculum development, and instructional technology. Operations is the next highest percentage of budgetary expenditures, followed by administration and student support services. Student support services involve expenses such as social work, guidance, health expenses, and psychological services.

148. C: The campus technology plan will include information such as when the computers were purchased, how they should be maintained, and when the computers should be replaced. If it is time to replace the computers, the school leader needs to identify what funds in the budget can be used to purchase new computers. If it is not time to replace the computers, the school leader may request technical support for improving the functionality of the computers.

149. B: Although a technology budget cut is bad news, the principal would want to assess the current technology equipment on campus first. If the campus is already technology rich, the budget cut may not result in a drastic impact to instruction for the upcoming school year and little to no action may be necessary. After assessing the current technology equipment on campus, the principal can determine if the equipment meets the needs for the upcoming school year and, if not, how to make adjustments.

150. A: Fundraisers are a common way for schools to secure money and resources outside of school budgets. Fundraisers should always be conducted within the policies and procedures outlined by the school campus and the school district.

151. D: School funding comes from a variety of sources, but for most states, the primary source of school funding is local property taxes. The federal government provides some funding, but this funding is usually unsubstantial and may fluctuate due to the changing budget decisions at the federal level. The state governments also provide funding to schools based on income and/or sales taxes, and for a minority of states, state funding can be the primary source of school funding. This is true for California, Hawaii, Michigan, New Mexico, Minnesota, Kansas, and Washington. The primary source of school funding in most states, however, is property taxes within the school district. Both residences and commercial properties are taxed, and a portion of those taxes are allocated to school districts. Schools and school districts often also seek grants and donations from foundations to supplement the school's budget.

152. C: To realize their school goals for students despite economic constraints, instead of the common but counterproductive school reactions of postponing improvements or cutting services and programs students need, school leaders can identify programs that are expensive but do not improve student performance while considering different alternatives for achieving the same results, like providing professional development less expensively by implementing study groups instead of paying for guest speakers and workshops.

153. D: Student growth is the best data point to inform the principal as to whether the reading program was effective. An effective program would result in individual and collective student growth as measured by a pre- and post-assessment. Feedback from students and teachers is valuable and can be considered in the budgeting decision; however, a principal would not want to purchase a program if it does not produce results, even if the students and teachers viewed the program positively.

154. A: The US Departments of Education's and Justice's school discipline guidance package intends to lower significant overall annual student expulsion and suspension rates, including disproportionate overrepresentation of students with disabilities and from other minorities. The package also aims to help schools establish positive learning environments *and* enhance school safety; to aid schools having difficulty establishing safe, positive learning environments, even though violent school incidents overall are less than before; and to ensure school behavioral interventions are both federally legal *and* non-discriminatory.

155. C: Community business owners and employees are included among stakeholders in education; however, the school leader is less likely to survey them than those more key to this particular topic, including the superintendent of schools, administrators in the central office (A), members of the local school board, parents of the students (B), the students themselves, the teachers, and the paraprofessionals working at the school (D).

156. C: Obeying federal, state, and local laws and regulations (II) and implementing the local board of education's administrative regulations and policies (V) could both conflict with acting to change laws and regulations that are against valid education goals (IV), or vice versa, as obeying and implementing laws, regulations, and policies can be countermanded by acting to change laws, regulations, or policies.

157. B: The Civil Rights Act of 1964 (A) protects everyone, including students, against discrimination for multiple reasons. The Americans with Disabilities Act (ADA, 1973) protects individuals against discrimination for disabilities; Title II of the ADA Amendments Act of 2008 (C) protects students with disabilities from discrimination by requiring equal opportunities to benefit from government programs, services, and activities, including education. Section 504 of the Rehabilitation Act of 1973, amended 2003 (D), also protects students with disabilities against discrimination. The 1974 Family Educational Rights and Privacy Act (FERPA) protects student education records privacy; the Individuals with Disabilities Act (IDEA) does this for students with disabilities (B).

158. A: The Individuals with Disabilities Education Act (IDEA) and Family Rights and Privacy Act (FERPA) both define the same document types as educational records (B). FERPA determines conditions for educational records destruction based on state laws (C). IDEA amendments regarding educational records collection, maintenance, confidentiality, disclosure (D), and destruction (C) are based on FERPA. However, the IDEA requires designating special education records custodians to ensure the instruction and training of all educators collecting confidential information, but FERPA does not (A).

159. C: Effective school leaders involve all students in developing systems for collecting, analyzing, applying, incorporating, and sharing data rather than only identifying some students to involve (A); involve all staff members in participating in developing assessment plans rather than designating certain members (B); involve students closely in knowing and monitoring their own data (C); and basing individual student goals on each student's specific data measures, not just on overall school data (D).

160. D: School leaders should not analyze only ethical implications of decisions for the school community (A) but habituate every member to such analysis to guide their approaches. Because total experience and learning contribute to their development, ethical frameworks should grow throughout school leaders' careers, not remain constant (B). Ethical school leaders never accept funding from donors requiring less effective methods (C). By regularly engaging staff and stakeholders in conversations helping them self-examine assumptions and develop ethical understanding (D), school leaders integrate ethical discussion into school culture.

161. A: From their direct involvement with schools and school districts, school leaders are most knowledgeable about educational issues; therefore, lawmakers need to hear from them about these issues to inform the bill they get passed. School leaders can lobby for their schools as individuals (B), or through community contacts (e.g., local businesses, community leaders, and local politicians), or through their professional organizations (C). The largest professional organizations for school administrators have their own registered lobbying staffs. School leaders need not be professional lobbyists (D) to influence legislators.

162. D: The National Education Association (NEA) Code of Ethics principle of Commitment to the Student prohibits *unreasonably preventing* students from independently pursuing learning and *unreasonably denying* student access to various perspectives, not encouraging these. It *requires*, not prohibits, reasonable efforts to safeguard students against harm to health, safety, or learning. It prohibits *suppressing*, not disclosing, any information pertinent to student progress. However, it does prohibit disclosing student information when not legally or professionally required.

163. C: It is not the school leader's responsibility to interpret federal and state law for application at the school level because this is the responsibility of the school district as articulated in local policy; however, the school leader is responsible for knowing federal and state law. School policies and local laws are developed in accordance with federal and state laws; however, if there is a discrepancy between local policies and federal or state law, the school leader must adhere to federal and state law. Policies are interpretation of law and must be revised and updated regularly to align with state and federal laws. School leaders are their own agents regarding voting in elections relating to policy.

164. B: As of 2013, New Jersey and Wyoming required *all* persons to report child abuse and neglect; all other US states identified specific professionals as mandated reporters. These professions include healthcare and mental health professionals *and* childcare providers; teachers, principals, and other school personnel; social workers, *including* school social workers; law enforcement officers; and medical examiners or coroners.

165. A: It is the responsibility of the school principal to establish and monitor the implementation of processes and procedures that protect students and the confidentiality of their information.. This breach of student confidentiality could have posed a safety risk of the student; the attendance clerk violated policy and law by providing the student's information over the telephone without verifying who they were speaking to. Even though the attendance clerk failed to adhere to policy, it is ultimately the principal's responsibility to ensure that all staff are trained on policies affecting student rights and confidentiality and adhere to those policies.

166. Essay question graders commonly look for the following elements in a strong response: strong content knowledge, clear organization, and effective arguments or examples. Language and usage are not usually strictly graded, but can make a big impact on the clarity of your ideas.

Please use the provided rubric to make sure your response meets these common criteria. Try to have a friend or family member grade your response for you or take a break after writing your response and return to grade it with fresh eyes.

Constructed Response Rubric

Domain	Description
Content Knowledge	• The response directly addresses every part of the prompt. • The response demonstrates independent knowledge of the topic. • The response discusses the topic at an appropriate depth.
Organization	• The response introduces the topic, usually with a thesis statement or by restating the prompt. • The response directly addresses the prompt by providing a clear and concise answer or solution. • The answer or solution is supported by logical arguments or evidence. • The response restates the main idea in the conclusion.
Arguments and Examples	• The response provides a reasonable answer to the prompt. • The answer is supported by strong reasoning or evidence. • The response develops ideas logically and connects ideas to one another. • The reasoning and evidence provided act to support a unified main idea.
Language and Usage	• The response demonstrates effective use of grammar and uses varied sentence structure throughout the response. • The response demonstrates correct use of spelling, punctuation, and capitalization. • The response demonstrates strong and varied use of vocabulary relevant to the topic and appropriate for the intended audience.

Practice Test #2

Leadership for Student Learning

1. Which of the following is true about mental health and student learning and achievement?

a. Educational problems are not related to mental health issues.
b. External stressors can create obstacles to learning and achievement.
c. Only psychological disorders diagnosed by a health professional can be addressed in schools.
d. Only students who qualify for special education services can receive support for mental health issues.

2. School leaders must know of a wide range of mental health professionals available to students. To which of the following are students most often referred for help that schools cannot provide?

a. Career counselors
b. Family counselors
c. Group counselors
d. School counselors

3. In terms of assessment, which of the following is a true statement that school leaders should consider when minimizing bias and maximizing equity for all students?

a. Accommodations given to students during testing are inherently unfair.
b. Progress monitoring using student data decreases achievement gaps.
c. Achievement gaps can be resolved by testing low performing students frequently and extensively.
d. Assessment validity and reliability nullifies most non-standardized test results.

4. An elementary school leader has set a goal of establishing a school climate wherein all educators believe every child can learn and succeed, and are committed to enabling every child to do so. Which classroom practice should the leader encourage teachers to use toward this goal?

a. Differentiating instruction
b. Assigning student teams to compete in contests
c. Differentiating assessment standards by student
d. Regularly researching individual student interests

5. In a manifestation determination meeting, if a school Individualized Education Program (IEP) committee determines a student's behavior was a manifestation of his or her disability, what correctly identifies an area the IEP committee will address through a suitable plan?

a. Modifying implementation of the IEP other than how it is written
b. Adding accommodations, services, etc.without changing the IEP
c. Offering additional services as needed without more evaluations
d. Making a functional behavior assessment to inform intervention

6. The dean of instruction analyzed data from the most recent benchmark assessment and noticed that when the data was disaggregated by race and ethnicity, a particular group failed to meet performance standards. How should the dean address this?

a. Talk to teachers who instruct the demographic group and students that belong to the demographic group to identify the challenges they are facing in mastering the content.
b. Contact the parents of the students who were not successful and inform them that their child needs tutoring.
c. Observe the teachers who instruct the demographic group to determine their efficacy.
d. Develop a schedule of tutorials and remediation for the students who did not master the content.

7. Among classroom assessment principles that school leaders must know for effective collaboration with teachers, which choice is MOST representative?

a. A few specific assessment instruments are error free.
b. Authors and users typically overestimate testing error.
c. Assessment reliability applies to tests, not test scores.
d. Good assessment is valid, reliable, ethical, and fair.

8. Educational research into collaborative data analysis has identified four areas. Which of these areas involves the process of exploring learning standards, goals, and definitions?

a. Calibration
b. Student data focus
c. Educator engagement
d. Supportive technology

9. What is the primary reason that curriculum and instruction must be aligned to assessments?

a. School leaders must be able to justify why they select curriculum and resources.
b. Teachers must know what to teach in the classroom.
c. Assessments that are not aligned with curriculum and instruction will not accurately measure what students learned.
d. Alignment of curriculum and assessments makes it easier to analyze and compare student performance data.

10. The sixth-grade math department meets as a professional learning community and determines that overall students in sixth-grade are not performing well on the same three math objectives. However, these same students are performing satisfactorily on other math objectives. Which of the following is the most likely reason that the sixth-grade students are not mastering the identified math objectives?

a. The math teachers are ineffective in teaching the identified math objectives.
b. The curriculum is not properly aligned to address the identified math objectives.
c. The students need additional tutoring to master the identified math objectives.
d. The assessment used to measure student performance was biased.

11. Which of the following is a primary benefit of professional learning communities?

a. They provide opportunities for teachers to share ideas.
b. They provide constructive feedback on student performance.
c. They identify areas in the curriculum that need revision.
d. They ensure that the standards-based curriculum is delivered.

12. The school principal institutes a professional learning community made up of social studies and reading teachers from grades six through eight. This professional learning community is an example of which of the following?

a. Horizontal alignment of curriculum and instruction
b. Vertical alignment of curriculum and instruction
c. Horizontal and vertical alignment of curriculum and instruction
d. Cross-cultural integration of curriculum and instruction

Refer to the following for question 13:

The school principal reviews classroom observation and feedback with assistant principals weekly but often has very few classroom observations of their own conducted in preparation for the weekly meeting. This week, a teacher complained to the principal that the feedback from their most recent evaluation was not fair because it did not provide a well-rounded view of their performance.

13. Other than classroom observations, which of the following would best provide an additional source of data for the principal to evaluate the teacher on?

a. Student performance data
b. Student surveys
c. Parent surveys
d. Teacher self-assessments

14. A school leader is monitoring the curricular programs to determine whether student needs are being met. Which of the following would provide the most valid indication that the curricular programs are meeting student needs?

a. Assessment data shows that students are meeting minimum performance standards.
b. Parent survey data demonstrates that parents are pleased with the curricular programs.
c. Teacher observations are generally positive.
d. Assessment data shows that most students are demonstrating academic growth.

15. A principal has received notice that the current standards will be phased out and a new set of standards will be adopted for the upcoming school year. Which of the following actions should the principal take first regarding curriculum development and revision?

a. Set aside money in the school budget for purchasing new curriculum.
b. Create a committee to advise the principal on curriculum adoption.
c. Plan dates for training teachers about the new curriculum.
d. Identify what standards are changing and how the current curriculum and resources align to the new standards.

16. Which of the following should be considered first when adopting curriculum?

a. Alignment to federal and state standards
b. Teacher approval
c. Community approval
d. Board approval

17. Which of the following is the best example of differentiated instruction based on product?

a. Teach different content for different students.
b. Allow students to choose between writing an essay or recording a video for an assignment.
c. Give students different version of assessments.
d. Assign some students to watch a video while others read an article.

18. Which of the following things can school leaders do to give teachers a safe environment for expressing their ideas?

a. Giving critical feedback about unusual ideas they express
b. Scheduling regular, brief meeting times for original ideas
c. Taking care not to let teachers undermine their authority
d. Asking them how "safe" differs for teachers versus students

19. Which of the following principles about formative assessment should school leaders consider when giving feedback to and collaborating with teachers?

a. Student motivation and learning are unaffected by assessment types.
b. Student motivation and learning are affected by assessment types.
c. Error is inevitable in all assessment, and only summative assessment is a valid indicator of student learning.
d. Student performance against a standard is more important than student growth.

20. A middle school principal wants to improve the quality of teaching and learning on campus on a continuous basis throughout the school year rather than only reviewing annual performance data and making changes prior to the start of the school year. Which of the following strategies would best help the principal to achieve this goal?

a. Assess students every six weeks using benchmark exams and use the data to adjust the instructional program.
b. At the start of the school year, administer a comprehensive exam to determine what information students retained over the summer.
c. Administer a comprehensive exam to students at the beginning of the school year, in the middle of the school year, and at the end of the school year and use the data to make plans for the following school year.
d. Require that teachers maintain portfolios for all students to demonstrate learning and growth over the course of the school year.

21. A school leader wants to become more involved in analyzing student work on campus. Which of the following actions should the school leader take to accomplish this goal?

a. Audit student work samples and discuss the student performance demonstrated with the teachers who assigned the work.
b. Monitor teacher grade books.
c. Host a science fair.
d. Mandate that teachers assess student learning using portfolios.

22. Which of the following strategies is least likely to improve teacher practice?

a. Conducting regular classroom observations and providing written feedback to teachers
b. Pairing novice teachers with an experienced teacher for peer coaching
c. Providing teachers with aggregated student performance data each grading cycle
d. Facilitating professional learning communities for teacher collaboration by grade level and by content area

23. Which of these is recommended for school leaders to plan classroom visits effectively for giving teachers useful observational feedback?

a. Completing a checklist during every classroom visit to ensure that feedback is systematic and standardized
b. Giving teachers individual, not collective, feedback
c. Making frequent, shorter walk-throughs across the school to give feedback to as many teachers as possible
d. Using statistics to observe trends and give individual teacher feedback based on the trends

24. In reference to the Supportive School Discipline Initiative (SSDI), former US Attorney General Eric Holder said a federal initiative to guide school disciplinary practices would "make schools safe, supportive and inclusive for all students" and would "keep America's young people safe and on the right path." How did he say it would do these things?

a. By making discipline less exclusionary
b. By divorcing discipline from civil rights
c. By getting data from resource officers
d. By referring discipline to peace officers

25. A newly appointed principal has been advised that the teachers on campus are disgruntled and resistant to change. Which of the following is the best action for the principal to take first to address this issue?

a. Send out a survey to all teachers to assess campus culture.
b. Meet with a focus group of teacher leaders and allow them to voice their concerns.
c. Hold an all-staff meeting and communicate the vision for the school.
d. Send an email to all teachers informing them of new policies and procedures.

26. The federal Supportive School Discipline Initiative (SSDI) issued a (2014) positive school discipline guidance package. Why did the US Department of Justice (DOJ) collaborate with the US Department of Education (ED) in producing this resource?

a. To make school discipline consistent with justice and correctional systems
b. To address inevitable student justice involvement by disciplinary exclusion
c. To ensure that Civil Rights Act titles prohibiting discrimination are enforced
d. To establish disciplinary practices to keep juvenile offenders out of school

27. Which of the following best defines equity?

a. Providing all students with the same amount of resources and support
b. Providing students with the resources and support that meet their individual needs
c. Providing at-risk students with additional resources and support
d. Providing accommodations for students who receive special education services

28. A middle school principal decides to select and train several lead teachers in the math department to conduct action research on campus. This decision is an example of which of the following strategies?

a. Providing teachers with the opportunity to take appropriate risks for improving teaching and learning
b. Encouraging collaboration between teachers to support professional growth
c. Using data-driven decision making to improve student performance
d. Giving teachers a voice in school decisions

29. A school leader is developing a plan for improving teaching on campus and has identified several effective teachers in the math department. How should the school leader best incorporate these teachers into the plan?

a. Request that the teachers mentor low-performing teachers.
b. Allow the teachers to continue teaching using their current best practices.
c. Recognize the teachers for their effective performance.
d. Allow the teachers to identify areas in which they would like to grow and provide resources and support.

30. Which of the following would most impact the success of a new teacher induction program?

a. Providing optional coaching sessions for new teachers
b. Assigning mentors to new teachers based on the seniority of the mentor teacher
c. Providing opportunities for collaboration and leadership development
d. The school leader facilitates all aspects of the induction program

31. Which of the following best represents a threat to a physically safe campus environment?

a. Inefficient arrival and dismissal procedures
b. High student-to-teacher classroom ratios
c. High teacher turnover
d. Electrical hazards

32. What is most accurate regarding social and emotional learning (SEL) programs that schools often offer in conjunction with school-wide positive behavior support (SPBS) programs?

a. Programming is implemented at individual grade levels
b. Programming requires quarterly monitoring
c. Programming includes practicing opportunities
d. Programming is limited to the school environment

33. An elementary school principal serves at a school in which many of the parents of students speak little or no English. The language barrier creates challenges in communication, parent engagement, and the reinforcement of learning at home. Which of the following actions would best help the principal to address this challenge?

a. Hire a translator to communicate with parents.
b. Partner with an adult ESL program in the community and offer free ESL classes on campus.
c. Translate all school documents to the languages of the parents.
d. Ask students to translate information for their parents.

34. In school-wide positive behavior support programs, which level typically involves school-wide practices that support positive behaviors for all students?

a. Tier 1
b. Tier 2
c. Tier 3
d. Tier 4

35. According to research related to the factors that contribute to the success of higher-performing public schools, which of the following is true?

a. The school leader is the single defining success factor.
b. School success is based on a complex set of interrelated factors.
c. Schools cannot be successful without additional funding.
d. Factors related to curriculum and instruction are the most important determinants of success.

36. A school leader wants to create a risk-taking environment for teachers where they feel comfortable improving their practices for teaching and learning. Which of the following actions should the school leader take to accomplish this goal?

a. Create a system of peer evaluations.
b. Allow teachers to choose their own professional development opportunities.
c. Create a digital data dashboard so teachers can share achievement data with one another.
d. Place a suggestion box in the teachers' lounge.

37. Which of the following is the best example of how school leaders can support teachers in developing their expertise and leadership skills?

a. School leaders should increase teachers' workloads to give them opportunity to demonstrate responsibility.
b. School leaders should develop all teachers in the same way to avoid building resentment among staff.
c. School leaders must create safe environments for teachers' risk-taking and creative ideas.
d. School leaders should limit how much authority to share with teachers to prevent diminishing their own authority.

38. Which of the following most accurately reflects how school leaders can identify and decrease educational and institutional bias and discriminatory practices?

a. Establish anti-discrimination rules and identify a campus leader to enforce them.
b. Establish an anti-discrimination policy and form a committee to find opportunities to learn about and promote other cultures.
c. Hire a culturally diverse leadership team and have them speak to staff and students about their cultures.
d. Include opportunities in the curriculum for students to learn about other cultures.

39. A school leader has recently been appointed to school principal of ABC Elementary School. Which of the following actions would best help the new principal learn more about the community that the school serves?

a. Research the community online.
b. Review student demographic and academic performance data.
c. Meet with a variety of stakeholders of the community.
d. Meet with current staff to ask questions about the community.

40. Which of the following strategies would be most effective for communicating with stakeholders who speak a different language?

a. Hire translators and provide translation machines at community events.
b. Hire a bilingual principal.
c. Translate all written communications.
d. Ask students to translate for their parents.

41. To implement the school vision and pursue the school goals, how should a school leader best invite others to share these commitments?

a. Identify members of the school staff with common perspectives to ensure cooperation.
b. Identify members of the school and community with common perspectives to attain consensus.
c. Identify members of the school and community with diverse perspectives to assure representation.
d. Identify members of the school staff with diverse perspectives to implement equitably.

42. Which of the following is the MOST effective strategy for a principal to communicate the school vision to school personnel?

a. Morning announcements
b. Sending a daily e-mail to staff
c. Attending community events
d. Meetings in one-way format

43. Which of the following is the best way that a school leader can ensure equitable treatment of students and staff?

a. Develop policies and procedures and adhere to them.
b. Create advisory committees with representatives from a variety of diverse demographics.
c. Create a diversity and inclusion statement for the school.
d. Address student and staff complaints swiftly.

44. The Council of Chief State School Officers (CCSSO) has set national Educational Leadership Policy Standards for school leaders to guide school communities in respecting individual worth and dignity. Which of the following is NOT specifically included among these standards?

a. Promoting staff professional growth
b. Students monitoring their own data
c. Assuring efficient school operations
d. Responding to community diversity

45. Which of the following pieces of information would be most relevant when determining how to differentiate instruction for students?

a. Previous academic performance, special needs (such as a physical or learning disability), and learning style
b. Previous academic performance, demographics, and socioeconomic status
c. Student interests, career goals, and grade point average
d. Student interests, parental input, and learning style

46. School assessment data has revealed that there is a slant to the distribution of the assessment scores. Among the findings, it is shown that there is a normal distribution of students with delays and average-performing students, but that higher-achieving students are nearly completely missing. This has been interpreted to mean that higher-achieving students need more support to challenge them appropriately. A school leader wants to develop professional learning communities (PLCs) to identify and support high-achieving students through rigorous instructional practices. The first step the leader has taken was to ask the school leaders and faculty to endorse this goal as a school purpose.

Which of the following steps does not directly support the plan to develop PLCs to support this goal?

a. School leaders form staff teams whose members collaborate in accomplishing goals that support specific delays.
b. School leaders assign teams to review recent assessment data to identify students who may be under-supported.
c. School leaders and staff teams identify both exemplary and struggling teachers.
d. School leaders hire external consultants to evaluate effectiveness of current practices.

47. A school principal would like to engage a variety of stakeholders to inform the development of the school mission and vision. Which of the following strategies would best accomplish this goal?

a. Host a school assembly to get feedback from the student body.
b. Distribute a survey to students, parents, staff, and community members.
c. Create a committee of teachers, students, and parents.
d. Meet with local business owners in the community.

48. Which statement is accurate about why classroom management systems are effective?

a. By making learning environments orderly, they enable student academic success.
b. They control student behavior rather than helping emotional-social development.
c. They work by increasing prosocial behavior rather than academic engagement.
d. They work by providing individualized intensive interventions for all students.

49. Which of the following is most accurate about effective and appropriate school and co-curricular activities to prepare high school students for college and careers?

a. Career and technical education can only be obtained in magnet or technical schools.
b. School partnerships with higher education institutions best prepare students for jobs.
c. Community-based and project-based learning prepare students for higher education.
d. High school curricula should be pertinent to student lives, communities, and cultures.

50. Several community members have expressed concern to the school principal about the rate of teen suicide and believe that the principal should be proactive in promoting the mental health and wellbeing of students on campus. The school leader believes this is a helpful suggestion. Which of the following would be the best action to take to address the community members' concern?

a. Write an article in the school bulletin about teen suicide.
b. Begin a counseling and wellness program on campus that refers students to community agencies and resources.
c. Hang posters in the school hallways promoting a 24-hour suicide hotline.
d. Ban social media use on campus to prevent cyberbullying.

51. A new student arrives from Switzerland, speaks French, and is enrolled in XYZ High School. The only languages spoken at the school are English and Spanish. Which of the following actions should the school leader take in order to accommodate the needs of this student?

a. Research Swiss culture.
b. Pair the student with a peer to help the student get acclimated.
c. Hire a translator to help communicate with the student during classes.
d. Meet with the student and their family to discuss their needs using a temporary translator if possible.

52. Which of the following best illustrates the connection between the school community and local education trends?

a. A school creates an internship program for students interested in working in the healthcare industry.
b. Recruiters from local colleges set up booths in the school cafeteria during lunch time to inform students about their school choices.
c. Graduates of the local community college mentor high school seniors.
d. A school offers a college math preparation course based on the math skills needed for success at the local community college.

53. Compared to majority rule and committees, what is a more salient characteristic of group consensus as a way of making collaborative educational decisions?

a. It is more time-efficient than these other methods.
b. It can undermine commitment for minority voters.
c. It is more thorough and hears all members' voices.
d. It may make member time and effort not worth it.

54. Which of the following practices best represents the least restrictive environment (LRE) for a student who receives special education services?

a. The student remains in a classroom with other students who receive special education services throughout the day, with the exception of ancillary classes.
b. The student attends classes with students who do not receive special education services, but reports to a special education teacher's classroom during independent practice of each core class.
c. The student reports to a special education teacher's classroom for math and reading only.
d. The student attends classes with students who do not receive special education services and classroom teachers provide modifications to the curriculum and/or accommodations to assist the student.

55. According to research findings, transformational school leaders are most effective in promoting organizational learning. Which of the following best reflects how they do this?

a. By demonstrating their high expectations for students
b. By demonstrating their high expectations for teachers
c. By modeling ongoing learning and providing opportunities for staff to learn from peers
d. By researching effective instructional practices and training staff to implement them

56. Which of the following best describes the relationship between school leadership and student outcomes?

a. School leadership is directly related to student outcomes.
b. School leadership is indirectly related to student outcomes.
c. School leadership is not related to student outcomes.
d. There is not enough research to determine the nature of the relationship.

57. Which of the following is an accurate statement about tiered behavior management systems used with classrooms and/or individual students?

a. Classroom behavior management systems should start at the beginning of the school year.
b. Individual programs for disruptive student behavior must start at the beginning of the school year.
c. Classroom behavior management systems are applied for a school year, not across grades.
d. If students know expectations early on, then classroom management systems can be faded.

58. What does the National Association of Secondary School Principals (NASSP) recommend regarding effectively using community support outside the school to promote student mental health (MH)?

a. Providing community service personnel in schools' comprehensive staff development is excluded.
b. Providing school staff training in promoting positive school-wide environments is found ineffective.
c. Providing school staff training in how to use mechanisms to refer students to community services is effective.
d. Providing training in early identification of MH disorders and risks excludes community staff in schools.

Refer to the following for question 59:

A new school principal administered a survey to school staff to assess the perceived culture of the school. The data from the survey showed that most of the staff felt that all ideas for the school came from the top and were forced down. The school principal wants to shift the culture and encourage staff to be innovative.

59. Of the following, how could the school principal best provide a safe environment for teachers to express their beliefs and ideas to help them feel more involved?

a. Schedule monthly one-on-one meetings with individual teachers.
b. Place a suggestion box in the teachers' lounge.
c. Administer an electronic survey to campus staff to obtain feedback.
d. Provide collaborative meeting time for teachers and meet with them regularly to discuss their ideas.

60. What have researchers found regarding the relationship between student academic self-concepts and student outcomes?

a. Students' academic self-concepts are correlated with success later in life.
b. Students' academic self-concepts are correlated with their academic achievement.
c. Students' academic self-concepts are correlated with socioeconomic status more than home settings.
d. Students' academic self-concepts are correlated with enrollment in smaller schools.

Organizational Development

61. Research shows that school leaders' time spent on which of these does not predict better student achievement?

a. Making evaluations
b. Class walkthroughs
c. Coaching teachers
d. Program development

62. What is the primary purpose of professional learning communities?

a. To hold teachers accountable
b. To make it easier to monitor teaching and learning
c. To facilitate collaboration among teachers
d. To set and achieve instructional goals

63. Which of the following is not accurate regarding school leaders' engagement of faculty and staff in ongoing self-assessment and improvement?

a. To encourage self-direction in improving, leaders should model self-assessment and improvement.
b. To encourage self-direction in improving, leaders should actively engage workers.
c. To encourage self-direction in improving, leaders should make learning accessible.
d. To encourage self-direction in improving, leaders should leave self-improvement up to employees.

64. A school leader has decided to hire an instructional coach to support the teachers' growth. Which of the following is the most likely result of this decision?

a. The instructional coach will help the leadership team supervise and evaluate teachers.
b. The instructional coach will make the decisions regarding professional development and training on campus.
c. Having an instructional coach will eliminate the need for professional development and training on campus.
d. The instructional coach will provide individualized support to teachers to help them grow.

65. Which of the following best describes rigorous instruction?

a. Curriculum and instruction that is challenging to students
b. Honors, advanced placement, and dual credit courses
c. Appropriate grading and feedback on student work
d. Teaching above student grade levels

66. An assistant principal is reviewing a reading teacher's gradebook and notices that the students have very few grades entered for the marking period. The assistant principal is concerned and plans on meeting with the reading teacher. Which of the following questions is most important for the assistant principal to ask the teacher during this meeting?

a. Are you aware of the grading policy in the faculty handbook?
b. How many grades do you plan on assigning for the marking period?
c. How do you document student mastery of objectives?
d. Do you need help with grading assignments?

67. A high school principal ensured that the campus was fully staffed with highly qualified teachers at least a month before the start of the school year. What is the primary benefit of this effort?

a. Teachers who are hired early have more time to prepare for the school year.
b. Personnel budgets must be submitted before the school year begins.
c. All teachers will have an opportunity to participate in trainings and professional development prior to the start of the year.
d. Teachers who are hired later in the year have classroom management issues.

68. What should school leaders keep in mind when integrating technology into standards-based curricula?

a. They should assign their teachers to write technology standards.
b. They cannot help students meet standards by using technology.
c. They do not need to require students to master technology standards.
d. They should focus on learning with technology, not learning about it.

69. Which instructional materials would most promote student reflection?

a. Textbook end-of-chapter study questions
b. Venn diagrams and other graphic organizers
c. Journals for students to write in regularly
d. Worksheets for exercising new learning

70. Which pedagogical shift best supports the integration of technology into instructional practice?

a. From homogenous student groups to heterogenous student groups
b. From learning passively to learning actively
c. From teacher-directed learning to student-paced learning
d. From lesson activities to project-based learning

71. Alternative high school principals Mohr and Dichter (2001) codified developmental stages that school staff undergo to become learning communities. Which stage is associated with the emergence of a sense of community?

a. The stage involving conflict
b. The honeymoon stage
c. The confusion stage
d. The mature stage

72. What trends in student achievement data would be the best indicator that there are problems in curriculum alignment?

a. Students perform well on campus-based tests but perform poorly on college entrance exams.
b. Students earn satisfactory grades on school report cards but perform poorly on standardized tests.
c. Students with disabilities perform poorly on campus-based tests.
d. Students who have a history of high academic performance show little to no growth on standardized tests.

73. Which of the following have education researchers identified as important regarding implementation of school-wide data initiatives??

a. More training opportunities and promotion of the data system in implementation are most effective.
b. Technology that supports data initiatives offers the answer to data use in schools.
c. Individual teachers utilize data technology systems more quickly and productively.
d. The success of a school data initiative is determined by the data system selected.

74. Which of the following actions best demonstrates collaboration with teachers to maintain an instructional program that delivers standards-based instruction?

a. Audit instructional materials used in the classroom, including worksheets and teacher-developed materials.
b. Compare student course grades to performance on standardized tests.
c. Engage in professional learning communities with teachers to contribute to planning discussions about the curriculum.
d. Survey teachers to obtain feedback about new curriculum options.

75. A school principal would like to develop a positive partnership with the school community. Which of the following actions would best help the principal to achieve this goal?

a. Publish a monthly school newsletter with reminders for important school events.
b. Host a student award ceremony each semester to highlight school and student successes.
c. Attend all school athletic events.
d. Send a survey to all community members to get their feedback on school performance.

76. Which of the following accurately describes cognitive and affective processes involved in school organizational learning and staff development?

a. Conversation and affirmation are cognitive; reflection and invitation are affective
b. Reflection and conversation are cognitive; affirmation and invitation are affective
c. Reflection and affirmation are cognitive; conversation and invitation are affective
d. Affirmation and invitation are cognitive; reflection and conversation are affective

77. What is most true about effective new teacher induction programs?

a. They should focus on supporting new teachers but not leaders.
b. They should give only new teachers professional development.
c. They should use self-assessments and reflection for teachers to measure performance.
d. They should improve student achievement via teacher efficacy.

78. Which of the following best describes how school leaders of more effective schools assign students to new (i.e., novice or beginning) teachers, compared to their more experienced colleagues?

a. In more effective schools, new teachers are assigned students with lower achievement.
b. In more effective schools, new teachers are assigned students with higher achievement.
c. In more effective schools, new teachers are assigned randomly relative to achievement.
d. In more effective schools, new teachers are assigned students with similar achievement.

79. Which of the following statements does not support standardized classroom practices and procedures?

a. Improving the cost-efficiency of school programs by reducing differentiation
b. Increasing the conformity to curricula within departments
c. Promoting safety throughout the school
d. Ensuring that students can expect the same teaching style from each teacher

80. A school leader would like to increase the use of differentiated instruction as an instructional strategy on campus. Which of the following actions would be most effective in achieving this goal?

a. Publicly recognize teachers who use differentiated instruction in the classroom.
b. Purchase books about differentiated instruction and distribute them to all teachers.
c. Model differentiated instruction during professional development sessions and monitor classroom implementation.
d. Hire an instructional coach that can train teachers how to use differentiated instruction in the classroom and evaluate their efficacy.

81. The school principal had a meeting unexpectedly cancelled and decided to use the free time to engage in activities on campus related to curriculum and instruction. Which of the following activities should the principal choose to engage in?

a. Assist with lunch duty.
b. Identify students to tutor in a small group.
c. Visit professional learning committees to engage in discussion regarding student progress.
d. Analyze student performance data from the most recent benchmark assessment.

Refer to the following for question 82:

A school leader has been hired as the new principal of a public elementary school. State standardized test scores in English Language Arts (ELA) across all fourth-grade classes in this school have steadily declined over the past several years. Scores in reading, listening, and speaking have all declined. Scores in writing started out the lowest and have dropped the most since. The new principal and all fourth-grade teachers are meeting to study samples of student compositions and discuss how to improve writing achievement.

82. The principal wants to assist the teachers in identifying the best instructional strategies to augment their students' ELA achievement. Which of the following pairs of data sets would most inform this assistance?

a. Fourth-grade students' reading levels; fourth-grade ELA instructional schedules
b. Demographic information on the students; the vision statement for the school
c. Fourth-grade teachers' years of experience; fourth-grade teachers' educations
d. Student standardized test data, disaggregated; state grade-level ELA standards

83. Which of these is NOT one of the purposes of rigorous and relevant curriculum design?

a. To challenge educator views on how students learn
b. To incorporate the instructional skills of the teacher
c. To impose a structure on existing instructional goals
d. To incorporate new and different instructional goals

84. Among tenets of the philosophy of differentiating instruction that are compatible with standards-based instruction, which is described correctly here?

a. The Zone of Proximal Development enables optimal learning.
b. Designed learning opportunities are superior to natural ones.
c. The activation of prior knowledge enhances relevance, not learning.
d. A sense of community aids social, not academic, development.

85. A high school teacher's Algebra II class includes some students learning independently, some progressing as fast as she could teach them, and some lacking prerequisite skills for the course. The teacher's dual goal is to help every student acquire a solid grasp of mathematics and also pass the standards exam. Which of the following practices help her achieve this?

a. Letting students discover curriculum skills to master instead of telling them
b. Devoting most small-group instruction time to students needing more help
c. Dividing classroom time among varied instructional groupings and activities
d. Focusing on introducing new concepts rather than prior student knowledge

86. Regarding data collection, recording, and submission for monitoring student progress and relating it to state assessments, which school leader responsibility to help faculty is MOST accurately described?

a. Deciding how often, and to whom, teachers submit data
b. Ensuring teachers collect data periodically, for example, quarterly
c. Having faculty aid one another with data-recording forms
d. Applying state-assigned rubrics to assessment for faculty

87. How must school leaders help faculty and other staff with curriculum and instruction to identify and meet student needs?

a. They oversee but do not participate in designing curriculum and instruction.
b. They review programs regularly to determine correct implementation only.
c. They help faculty and staff meet unmet needs rather than implement plans.
d. They help faculty and staff identify content and practices to address needs.

88. When school principals collaborate with others in making curriculum decisions, who else should be involved?

a. Curriculum specialists and professional personnel
b. Curriculum specialists, professionals, and board members
c. The students and the school's professional personnel
d. School professionals and members of the board of education

89. What best describes knowledge of instructional practices that school leaders must have?

a. Helping teachers learn new methods but not predicting how long it will take
b. Knowing the time effective planning takes regardless of the number of students
c. Implementing new approaches, more importantly than networking teachers
d. Knowing the time effective planning takes according to the levels of content

90. School leaders can organize teachers into data inquiry teams to identify and address student academic needs. Which of the following most accurately describes the school leader's role in directing these teams?

a. Develop action plans according to data analyses.
b. Support the implementation of the action plans.
c. Analyze data from summative assessments only.
d. Analyze data by classes, not individual students.

91. A school leader and the leadership team have begun developing a plan for implementing the school goals. The leader has identified the necessary action steps, the persons responsible for each step, and the time frames in which each step should be taken. Which of the following is the most appropriate next step for finalizing the plan?

a. Identify the resources needed for each step and evidence of implementation.
b. Share the plan with persons who will be responsible for completing an action step.
c. Present the plan to staff.
d. Plan future meetings with staff to monitor progress in implementing the plan.

92. A new middle school principal is concerned about the academic performance of seventh-grade students in math. Which of the following actions should the principal take first when developing a plan to improve students' math scores?

a. Identify the curriculum, resources, and instructional strategies currently in use.
b. Allocate funding for math tutors.
c. Reassign struggling students to stronger teachers.
d. Administer additional math assessments to identify student weaknesses in math.

93. The PTO president expressed concern to the school principal about the recent announcement to purchase new science curriculum for ninth and tenth-grade students. He expressed that there was a greater need for college preparation materials for students. Which of the following responses from the principal is best?

a. Purchasing science curriculum was the economic choice because it will benefit a greater number of students for a smaller cost.
b. College preparation materials will be considered for purchase for the upcoming school year.
c. Student performance data demonstrates that students are already performing at a satisfactory level on college entrance exams.
d. One of the school goals for the year is to improve student performance in science and the curriculum purchase supports that goal.

94. Which of the following is the best way to identify strategies for facilitating change?

a. Host student and teacher focus groups to solicit suggestions and ideas.
b. Conduct pilot programs and collect data to determine efficacy.
c. Study research-based and proven best practices.
d. Meet with community stakeholders to solicit suggestions and ideas.

95. A goal for XYZ High School is to increase teachers' and students' technology skills. Which of the following decisions best demonstrates that the leader is aligning resources to achieve the goal?

a. Require all staff communications to be paperless.
b. Purchase updated computers for teachers and students and provide training for using them.
c. Conduct regular professional development for teachers related to technology skills.
d. Offer a new course to students that teaches basic computer skills.

96. Which of the following sources of data would be most beneficial for a school leader to analyze prior to developing or revising the school vision and goals?

a. Teacher turnover data, failure rates, and satisfaction survey results
b. Student performance data, student attendance data, and student promotion rates
c. Community engagement rates
d. School accountability ratings for the last three years

97. A school leader has developed the vision and goals in collaboration with the campus leadership team and community stakeholders. Which of the following is the best step that the school leader should take next?

a. Develop a strategic plan for implementing the vision and goals.
b. Host a community meeting to present the vision and goals to all stakeholders.
c. Delegate tasks to leadership team members to implement the vision and goals.
d. Host a meeting with campus staff to present the vision and goals and inform them of their duties and responsibilities related to the vision and goals.

98. Which of the following is the best evidence of effective monitoring of progress toward the vision and goals?

a. The leader implements clear checkpoints and milestones for goal activities.
b. The leader provides regular updates to stakeholders regarding progress toward the vision and goals.
c. Student performance data shows evidence of growth.
d. An advisory committee meets regularly to provide feedback to the leader regarding the vision and goals.

99. When utilizing school data to inform school vision, mission, and goals, which of the following data should school leaders analyze?

a. Historical data from standardized tests
b. Data from formative assessments
c. Course grades, promotion, and retention rates
d. Data from formative and summative assessments and community survey results

100. Which of the following does not pertain to the development of a shared school vision?

a. Ensuring that the vision is applicable to the whole community
b. Hosting community meetings to communicate the school vision
c. Surveying community members to receive insight
d. Collecting data to support an ideal outcome

101. A school leader is managing a significant structural change on campus. Which of the following strategies would be most effective in managing change?

a. Develop goals related to the new changes.
b. Obtain buy in from stakeholders by allowing them to have input.
c. Provide professional development opportunities that will equip teachers to be successful with the new changes.
d. Replace staff who are not on board with the changes.

102. A school's crisis response plan includes a "command and control" framework identifying personnel responsible for directing crisis response. What must school leaders assure most to make this aspect of the plan as effective as possible?

a. Select longest-term employees with the most familiarity of school operations. .
b. During a crisis, distribute leadership of command and control among several members.
c. Clearly define responsibilities for each identified member in advance for various crises.
d. During a crisis, have each command and control member report to at least two others.

103. Which of the following criteria would best help a school leader to determine if the school vision and goals are appropriate?

a. The vision and goals address the areas of deficit determined by analysis of multiple sources of data.
b. The vision and goals are approved by community stakeholders.
c. The vision and goals reflect a balance of the school's strengths and weaknesses.
d. The vision and goals mirror those established by schools with similar performance history and student demographics.

104. Which of the following strategies would most likely encourage stakeholders to support and implement the school vision and goals?

a. Announcing the school vision and goals at a community meeting.
b. Publishing the school vision and goals on the school website.
c. Including internal and external community members in the development of the vision and goals.
d. Selecting representatives from the staff and community to be advocates for the school's vision and goals.

105. A school leader is developing a process for continuous improvement on campus. Which of the following actions should the school leader take first?

a. Develop evaluation procedures and set checkpoints for evaluation.
b. Train staff on the continuous improvement process.
c. Select a low performing area that needs to be addressed.
d. Identify strategies for addressing low performing areas.

106. A school leader conducts a needs assessment for the school using student academic performance data, student attendance data, student focus groups, and teacher focus groups. The leader then decides to conduct an anonymous survey of community stakeholders. The primary benefit of this action is that:

a. The leader will increase buy in from the community.
b. Surveying the community will increase community engagement.
c. The school leader will be able to explain past school performance.
d. The school leader will have multiple sources of data to conduct a thorough needs assessment.

107. A school leader wants to enlist support for change on campus. Which of the following actions should be taken first?

a. Communicate the intended change effectively to all stakeholders.
b. Create an advisory committee.
c. Find supporters with influence over other stakeholders to help spread the word about the change.
d. Administer an anonymous survey to see how stakeholders feel about the proposed change.

108. Some successful school leaders have obtained public and financial support for their schools by communicating with community members. Which example of this is most applicable?

a. Sharing real estate data with the business community is unrelated to school success.
b. Local families are drawn to schools more by physical changes than better test scores.
c. Significant improvements for minority students are best shared within the first year.
d. Leaders should share substantial, overall school academic gains with families yearly.

109. Which of the following accurately reflects evaluative criteria that school leaders should consider first when deciding to utilize community resources to support student learning?

a. Congruence with the school's vision and mission
b. Immediate impact on student achievement
c. Results from prior implementation
d. The relationship of the person or organization to the school

110. Which of the following would be the most effective way to engage parents in student behavior management systems?

a. Distribute the behavioral code of conduct to parents at the beginning of the school year.
b. Find parent volunteers to help enforce the behavioral code of conduct.
c. Ask for feedback from parents on the draft of the behavioral code of conduct before it is finalized.
d. Develop a behavioral code of conduct in partnership with teachers, parents, and students.

111. What does research into school mental health show about collaboration with the community?

a. Clinical psychiatric care and other services are not practicable or suitable in schools.
b. A cohesive continuum of intervention must primarily address severe mental health problems.
c. School staff must work with families and service providers rather than policymakers.
d. An integrated intervention continuum must mainly address universal student need.

112. What is a result of school leaders' community outreach for partnerships with schools?

a. Community partners are more informed about schools, but do not feel ownership.
b. Community partners who personally help students learn do not expect any thanks because of mutual benefits.
c. Community access to school facilities only benefits the community, not the school.
d. Community members understand schools better by accessing their facilities and events.

113. The National PTA identifies factors promoting family school involvement as a critical form of stakeholder collaboration. Which factor(s) is/are more the responsibility of school leaders than the collective responsibility of school leaders, faculty, and staff?

a. Supporting the parenting skills of the parents or guardians of the students
b. Actively participating in and encouraging parental involvement in student learning
c. Engaging students' parents to become partners for school decision making
d. Community outreach, encouraging family volunteers, and serving on PTAs

114. Which of the following is a valid reason for a school to collaborate with external mental health services?

a. To provide school-age children in the United States with a variety options of mental health service providers
b. When services like clinical psychiatric care are infeasible and inappropriate to provide in the school context
c. When students and parents express that they are more comfortable with services that take place in the community instead of with school settings and staffs
d. When data demonstrates that a school's students are less likely to seek counseling services in schools

115. Regarding family involvement in educational decision making for their children, which of these statements is LEAST accurate?

a. Families are important to collaboration as their children's primary advocates.
b. Families are inspired to participate by the minority of families who volunteer.
c. Families can advocate for other families as aspects of school-based dialogues.
d. Families can provide service and support in developing learning communities.

116. School leaders are finding that communicating with the media helps them engage the public in education. Researchers find this public engagement reinforces community pride. What else do they find it does?

a. It has no effects upon local safety or security.
b. It increases public criticism of school reforms.
c. It helps the schools rather than communities.
d. It increases service to the school and community.

117. Measures of the effects of school community engagement strategies include changes in the behaviors and attitudes of parents, families, community members, and students. What represents some of these impacts on students?

a. Greater school achievement and fewer school behavior problems
b. Greater school attendance despite the same school enrollment
c. Greater school enrollment but not necessarily school achievement
d. Greater school achievement, although not necessarily satisfaction

118. In seeking community support and additional resources, how do effective school leaders communicate with prospective partners?

a. Define how school leaders' needs and stakeholders' wants can coincide.
b. Speak reactive language when communicating with business executives.
c. Identify business or organization visions exactly matching school visions.
d. To motivate prospective partners, explain how schools will benefit.

119. Which of the following would be most likely to cause an administrator to look for outside resources in assisting students and their families?

a. A student is having difficulty in math class.
b. Two students participated in a physical altercation.
c. A student and his or her family are struggling financially and are in need of food and clothing.
d. A student will be the first in the family to graduate high school.

120. Which of the following strategies is most effective for communicating school and student success to families and the community?

a. Publishing a monthly school newsletter
b. Sending weekly automated calls
c. Sending letters home with students
d. Hosting monthly community meetings

Systems Leadership

121. Which of the following statements correctly reflects considerations for school leaders in supporting school improvement through effective resource management?

a. The school vision and goals are most dependent upon physical resources.
b. Material resources are priority as they are needed for a safe, comfortable teaching and learning environment.
c. Fiscal resource management is necessary for managing other resources, with some exceptions.
d. Human resource management is necessary for smaller class sizes and optimal student learning and achievement.

122. According to experts, applying systems thinking to school organizations results in which of these characteristics?

a. Policies and practices of school systems are improved continuously.
b. Curricula become diversified within the school system.
c. School systems become independent of other community systems.
d. Priorities are identified for the success of targeted student groups.

123. When leaders advocate for their schools in writing, which kind of writing skills do they need to recount true success stories about school initiatives and programs?

a. Persuasive writing skills
b. Descriptive writing skills
c. Narrative writing skills
d. Expository writing skills

124. Among school leader responsibilities for managing daily school facility operations, which is MOST likely to involve district support for hiring expert consultants to address contemporary issues?

a. Managing the food services in the school
b. Managing school environmental quality
c. Managing school transportation services
d. Managing custodial services in a school

125. Which of the following criteria would make a school the best candidate for implementing an integrated management system as new technology for managing school operations?

a. The school has not been using any digital management system.
b. The school has been using one management system with no plans for more.
c. The school has one or more systems and plans on adding more systems.
d. The school wants separate system policies and documentation.

126. What correctly represents National Education Association (NEA) guidelines for school acceptable use policies (AUPs) regarding classroom Internet technology?

a. It should have a policy statement including covered computer services and student use conditions.
b. It should have a definition section covering important terms used, but a preamble is not necessary.
c. It should include a section that defines acceptable use, but not one that defines unacceptable use.
d. It should include a violations or sanctions section, which should only define violations of the policy.

127. A principal is planning for the upcoming school year. Which of the following factors would most directly impact student learning?

a. The number of math and reading teachers on staff and the size of the classes that they teach
b. The benchmark testing schedule for the academic year
c. The time that school starts each day
d. The number of computers purchased

128. According to the federal government, the core components of a response strategy to information system threats and breaches are policy, plan, and procedure. Which of the following is a function of the policy component?

a. Defining staff responsibilities and mechanisms for remediation
b. Identifying needed management support and school resources
c. Standardizing response tasks and behaviors and averting errors
d. Conducting risk assessments on a regular basis as a preparation

129. School emergency response team organization is modeled after the Incident Command System (ICS) of Homeland Security's National Incident Management System (NIMS). Main ICS functions include Finance. Which of the ICS Management Systems identifies services and resources to support incident response needs?

a. Logistics
b. Planning
c. Command
d. Operations

130. Developing a school safety plan requires the participation of which of the following and for which reason?

a. School leaders and staff, because only they know their school and students best
b. School personnel only, because schools are for controlling as well as for learning
c. The entire community, because school crime data reflect community crime data
d. Law enforcement and mental health professionals, because they address crimes

131. Nationally, public-school districts receive the largest proportion of funding from which of the following sources?

a. Federal government
b. Their city government
c. The state government
d. Various other sources

132. Who typically makes student enrollment projections for determining school budgets?

a. District Offices of Achievement and Accountability alone project the student enrollments
b. District Offices of Achievement and Accountability with school leader revision as needed
c. The school leader alone projects the student enrollments for his or her school every year
d. Final projections are by committees from the district finance and student support offices

133. Which of the following describes the school district policy to allow principals autonomy to spend their campus budget as they see fit?

a. Local school management
b. Hybrid financial decision-making
c. Budgetary autonomy
d. Decentralization

134. A math intervention program that was implemented on a high school campus for the previous school year was funded by a grant that is expired. The principal must determine whether to fund the program using the local budget or to eliminate the program. Which of the following data points would best inform the principal as to whether the math intervention program should continue to be funded?

a. Student attendance in the program
b. Feedback from students regarding the program
c. Student math performance data from the beginning of the school year compared to the end of the school year
d. Student performance on the state mandated assessment for the previous school year

135. The campus technology coordinator recommends to the principal that new desktop computers be purchased for three of the campus's computer labs. The dean of instruction recommends that classroom technology should be upgraded first. Which of the following strategies should the principal implement first to decide how to prioritize these recommendations in the school's technology budget?

a. The principal should physically inspect the current equipment to determine which is in the most need of replacement.
b. The principal should refer to the campus improvement plan to determine how the recommendations align with the vision and goals for the school.
c. The principal should seek donations from stakeholders to assist with improving technology across the campus.
d. The principal should determine which of the recommendations is most economical.

136. A high school principal determines that it is no longer financially viable to sponsor the fine arts program at the school. Enrollment in fine arts courses has steadily decreased over the past four school years and the expenses of the program have exceeded the budget. However, the principal knows that many stakeholders in the community feel strongly about having a fine arts program. Which of the following represents the best action for the school principal?

a. Continue to offer the fine arts program.
b. Make an announcement to the students and staff that there will not be a fine arts program next year.
c. Host a fundraiser for the fine arts program.
d. Host a meeting to explain to stakeholders the reasons for eliminating the fine arts program.

137. Fire code regulations mandate that a fire drill should be conducted on campus monthly. It is the last day of the month and the principal realizes that a fire drill has not yet been conducted for the month. However, students are taking a mock standardized assessment. What action should the principal take?

a. Conduct the fire drill immediately.
b. Contact the fire inspector and inform them that the school was unable to conduct a fire drill for the month.
c. Document why the fire drill was not conducted for the month and provide the documentation if requested.
d. Contact the fire inspector to request an exception for the month.

138. A leader must ensure that the school's physical plant, equipment, and support systems operate safely, efficiently, and effectively. Which of the following strategies best helps the school leader fulfill this responsibility?

a. Walking the campus two times a day to check for safety
b. Soliciting feedback about the campus from teachers and staff
c. Selecting the appropriate staff to manage the physical plant
d. Reviewing all inspection reports monthly

139. Which of the following is the best example of a school leader utilizing technology to support effective school organization management?

a. Using technology to reconcile the budget and coordinate facility operations
b. Using technology to text message and email stakeholders about meetings
c. Using technology to collect, disaggregate, and analyze different school data
d. Using technology to facilitate multiple stakeholder contributions to projects

140. Which of the following does not demonstrate that an education leader proactively addresses challenges to student emotional safety?

a. The education leader collaborates with the school counselor to design a referral system for students experiencing an emotional or mental crisis.
b. The education leader provides information about free resources in the community for mental health needs to all parents and stakeholders at the beginning of the school year.
c. The education leader creates a grief counseling group following the suicide of a student.
d. The education leader schedules a counselor to visit the school monthly.

141. A school is in the process of implementing a campus-wide adoption of new technology. Which of the following is LEAST central to the role of a school leader acting to implement this change?

a. Leading by example and using technology with teachers and students
b. Attending professional development classes and keeping current with the research
c. Establishing conditions for change by setting high learning expectations and encouraging teacher effort
d. Encouraging use of the new technology, offering teachers learning opportunities, and resolving implementation problems

142. According to some school consensus-building models, which of these is most typical?

a. One hundred percent of faculty must agree to implement what is proposed 100 percent of the time.
b. Dissenting members can opt out of the implementation.
c. If consensus seems impossible, having 80 percent of members agree is not enough.
d. Those dissenting must agree not to obstruct and to support implementation.

143. Among the following personnel who may work in a public school, which of the following would likely be campus-based personnel?

a. A bus driver
b. A school counselor
c. A food service worker
d. A school psychologist

144. Which of the following is true about the efficacy of new teacher induction programs on schools?

a. They make new teachers more comfortable, not more effective.
b. They increase the rates at which the new teachers are retained.
c. They enhance teacher instructional skills, not teacher leadership.
d. They help education inequities more than student achievement.

145. Which of the following best describes how the school leader should evaluate the technology data systems they use?

a. Does the data system provide the data necessary to support the work of collaborative data teams?
b. Is the technology data system affordable?
c. Is the technology data system user friendly?
d. Do other schools use this technology data system?

146. When school leaders and school district personnel plan school budgets according to budget allocations issued by their school district, which of the following is correct?

a. It is most difficult to project employee salaries for the next school year.
b. Employee benefits are more difficult to predict than employee salaries.
c. Transportation expenses are included in budgets as these are essential.
d. School districts cannot reserve funds for unplanned emergency repairs.

147. A principal has led the school in applying databases, word processing programs, spreadsheet programs, and other application software to solve problems, manage information, and create sophisticated products. This is most related to which purpose of technology use in schools?

a. Using technology as a productivity tool
b. Using technology as information access
c. Using technology as a cognitive stimulus
d. Using technology as instruction content

148. Regarding acceptable use policies (AUPs) for student Internet access in public schools, which statement is most applicable?

a. The most important factor is the fundamental right of Americans to information access.
b. School district AUPs always require student agreement and parental permission forms.
c. A workable school AUP should achieve a balance between freedom and responsibility.
d. Schools should not consult outside organizations about digital freedom of information.

149. For managing school food services, the FDA refers to seven Hazard Analysis and Critical Control Point (HACCP) principles. Which of the following lists these principles in the correct sequence?

a. Identifying CCPs, determining critical limits to control hazards, hazard analysis, planning corrective actions, establishing CCP monitoring procedures, record-keeping system, verification procedures.
b. Hazard analysis, identifying CCPs, determining critical limits to control hazards, establishing CCP monitoring procedures, planning corrective actions, verification procedures, record-keeping system.
c. Verification procedures, determining critical limits to control hazards, identifying CCPs, establishing CCP monitoring procedures, hazard analysis, record-keeping system, planning corrective actions.
d. Determining critical limits to control hazards, identifying CCPs, establishing CCP monitoring procedures, verification procedures, record-keeping system, planning corrective actions, hazard analysis.

150. Regarding school buildings and grounds maintenance, for which of these are school leaders directly responsible?

a. Inspection and maintenance procedure development
b. Allocation of budget for inspection and maintenance
c. Inspection and maintenance schedules development
d. Preventive maintenance procedures implementation

151. In a school's Acceptable Use Policy (AUP) for classroom Internet technology, which section is MOST likely to cross-reference or even duplicate the general school disciplinary code?

a. Violations and sanctions
b. Acceptable uses
c. Unacceptable uses
d. Policy statement

152. Which of the following is a benefit of having a centralized budget within a district?

a. Increased flexibility in meeting the individual needs of students and classes
b. Increased buy in from school leaders and staff members
c. Improved financial coordination between different campuses
d. More efficient control and tracking of expenses

153. Related to school safety plans, goals for school leaders include which of these?

a. Leading school needs assessments, safety plan development, and implementation monitoring
b. Developing a system to monitor school incidents and crime that others share with stakeholders
c. Appointing personnel to design safe traffic patterns inside and outside the school environment
d. Adopting emergency evacuation procedures and delegating crisis management procedure choices

154. Among responsibilities of the school leader related to the school emergency plan are to conduct emergency response drills, evaluate staff responses, and revise the plan based on the results. These activities apply to which phase of emergency management?

a. Preparedness
b. Prevention
c. Response
d. Recovery

155. A high school principal has been invited by a community leader to participate in a community event in which the principal will have a brief opportunity to address the community. Of the following, which information would be most important to share with the community stakeholders at this event?

a. Provide information on how to sign up to be a volunteer at the school.
b. Recruit volunteers and mentors for at-risk students.
c. Provide updates on progress toward the school vision and goals.
d. Describe opportunities to collaborate with businesses in the community.

156. Which of the following is accurate about the uses of data in goal-related activities?

a. Qualitative data is not useful when setting goals aligned with school vision and mission.
b. Data connected to vision and mission enable monitoring progress for goals.
c. Only formative data is relevant to how schools allocate resources to meet their goals.
d. Formal data collection is not necessary to assess family and community relations.

157. A new principal hosts a meeting with community stakeholders to share ideas about the new vision and goals for the school. One of the community members insists that the school focus on improving the school's fine arts program. Which of the following should the new principal consider before including the fine arts program in the vision and goals for the school?

a. How many students are currently participating in the fine arts program?
b. Does the school have the appropriate staff to implement a successful fine arts program?
c. Does focusing on the fine arts program align with district, state, and federal policies and accountability standards?
d. Does the school have the financial resources to support an expanded fine arts program?

158. When using student outcome data to monitor school improvement progress, which of these would indicate a need to update the school improvement plan?

a. Data show improvement goals taking longer to be met than planned.
b. Data show that the school is on target to meet expected goals.
c. Data can be monitored more frequently due to acquisition of improved technology applications.
d. Data show that the school lags behind other schools with similar student populations.

159. Regarding how school leaders involve students appropriately in school improvement teams and processes, which of the following is true?

a. Planning school-wide forums is always a school leader's job
b. Some students have conducted school-wide survey research
c. Students have never participated in hiring any school leader
d. Students testifying in the state legislatures is against the law

160. Which of the following is the most crucial question to consider when developing school goals?

a. Are the school goals based on accurate data?
b. Are the school goals achievable?
c. Are the school goals aligned with the school vision?
d. Were stakeholders given the opportunity to participate in the development of the school goals?

161. The math teachers on campus suggest to the school leader that improved academic performance in math should be one of the school's goals. The school leader agrees and decides to create a measurable goal for student math performance. Which of the following is the best example of a measurable math performance goal?

a. 95% of eighth-grade students will demonstrate growth in their math class.
b. All eighth-grade students will be successful in their math class.
c. Eighth-grade students will earn at least a B average in their math class.
d. 90% of eighth-grade students will earn at least a B average in their math class.

162. How should school leaders and others analyze school data to inform the school vision?

a. Across grade levels instead of across school years
b. By subject matter rather than by student cohorts
c. By formative and summative assessment findings
d. By teachers within grades instead of across levels

163. Of the following, which is an advantage of developing a school vision collaboratively?

a. Visions developed through collaboration can be implemented far faster.
b. Visions are clearer and more coherent when developed by collaboration.
c. Visions take longer times in the process of development, slowing change.
d. Visions tend to be more appropriate to their local school district contexts.

164. Which of the following statements is not accurate about requirements for integrating technology comprehensively into instruction to support school vision?

a. Successful school-wide implementation of educational technology is dependent on the technology selected, not school leadership.
b. Regardless of the technology capabilities of school staff, training and professional development are needed to successfully implement educational technology school-wide.
c. School structure and organization impact the success of adopting educational technology.
d. Schools must have the resources and support for implementing technology school-wide.

165. In school change processes, which of these is an example of a first-order change?

a. Forming a different approach to instruction
b. Forming new interactions and relationships
c. Forming site-based school advisory councils
d. Forming a sense of collaborative ownership

166. A group of parents have become increasingly disruptive at basketball games at the high school where you are the principal. There has been swearing, yelling, derogatory comments, etc. from the home bleachers. In 150-300 words, discuss how this situation could escalate, causing serious problems for the school, and outline the steps you would take to prevent this from happening.

Answer Key and Explanations for Test #2

Leadership for Student Learning

1. B: External stressors can create short-term or long-term obstacles for student learning and achievement and can lead to or be evidence of mental health issues. Not all student mental health issues or crises carry an official diagnosis; however, educators can provide support and resources for the symptoms that students display. Furthermore, students with diagnosed mental health issues may be provided support and resources through a 504-education plan in addition to or in lieu of an individualized education plan. Additionally, educators can offer resources and support to students with mental health issues who do not receive services under either program.

2. B: Students having family issues, or personal problems whose treatment involves family, are referred to family counselors. Group counseling promotes social skills and healthy interaction and can be provided within the school environment when the groups are selected with intention. Career counselors can help students choose career paths and preparation. Career counseling is often performed in schools by guidance counselors and others, making referrals infrequent.

3. B: Testing accommodations for some students based on their individual needs are not unfair, but actually make assessments fairer and also more valid. School leaders can help decrease achievement gaps among student cultural groups and backgrounds by using student data to monitor progress regularly. However, extensive testing of students, especially to the impediment of instruction, can be detrimental to students who are already low performing. Data collected from assessments, even non-standardized formative assessments, can be used to monitor student progress and inform instructional decisions.

4. A: Implementing differentiated instruction helps teachers to meet students where they are based on performance, learning style, and other student characteristics. Instruction can be differentiated based on lesson delivery, student activities, and student assessment. However, standards are often standardized and must remain the same for students as all students are expected to learn and succeed. Teachers can provide individualized resources and support to help students to meet those needs.

5. D: If the Individualized Education Program (IEP) committee determines a student's behavior was a manifestation of their disability, the school cannot expel the student or apply the same disciplinary procedures indicated for students without disabilities. The IEP committee's plan will address any or all of these areas: ensuring the IEP is consistently implemented as it is written; changing the IEP to include accommodations, services, etc. as needed; further evaluations to identify additional services that may be needed; and/or functional behavior assessment to inform interventions.

6. A: Cultural diversity can affect academic achievement of students for a variety of reasons, including language barriers, cultural bias in curriculum, cultural bias in instructional practices, and much more. If a particular demographic of students is not succeeding, the school leader must identify what the barriers to achievement are by talking with teachers, students, parents, and even community members. The school leader must then address those barriers by engaging diverse team members to meet the needs of all students on campus.

7. D: To collaborate effectively with teachers regarding assessment, school leaders must know classroom assessment principles, including that no assessment instrument is error free (A)—that is, all assessment involves some error; that authors and users of assessments typically underestimate testing error (B); that reliability, that is, getting consistent results across repeated administrations, applies to test scores and not the tests themselves (C); and that good assessment is not only valid (tests what it means or claims to test) and reliable but also ethical and fair (D).

8. A: Calibration is the process of exploring and reaching consensus about learning standards, goals, and definitions at building, system-wide, and district-wide levels. Student data focus (B) yields in-depth information, for example, how well students are meeting specific, time-limited learning objectives. Educator engagement (C) alleviates faculty mistrust under external accountability pressures and facilitates systemic, sustainable change. Supportive technology (D) facilitates teacher access to data and shares reciprocal support with data team collaboration.

9. C: Curriculum and instruction must be aligned to assessment because what is taught must be measured and what is measured must be taught. If instruction is not aligned to the assessment, it is likely that there will be no measurement of how well students mastered what was taught. Additionally, if instruction is not aligned to the assessment, it is likely that students will be assessed on concepts and material that they have not been taught. Neither of the scenarios is fair or beneficial to students.

10. B: Given that students were consistently performing well in math with the exception of three specific math objectives indicates that there is an issue with the curriculum being used to teach those objectives. Factors such as teacher quality or biased assessments would negatively impact student performance in all objectives, not just a select few and performance would vary from student to student. The most likely reason for students consistently underperforming in the same area despite being taught by different teachers is a misalignment of curriculum to the assessment of the objectives.

11. D: One of the foundations of a professional learning community is identifying the standards and curriculum that must be taught and ensuring that the curriculum is delivered effectively. A question that PLC members must ask is "What do we want students to learn?". Answering this question ensures that the standards-based curriculum is prioritized, and that formative and summative assessment is a reflection of the curriculum that is taught.

12. C: The PLC will include teachers in the same grade level in different subjects which is horizontal alignment. The PLC will also include teachers in different grade levels in the same subject which is vertical alignment. Consequently, this PLC is an example of both horizontal and vertical alignment of curriculum and instruction.

13. A: Student performance data is a valuable source of data for determining teacher efficacy. Effective instruction should result in student academic growth and satisfactory performance. Survey data and self- assessments can inform support and professional development for teachers but are not as useful in teacher evaluations due to their qualitative and subjective nature.

14. D: Effective curricular programs will help students grow academically. Meeting academic performance standards may not be a good indicator of appropriate curricular programs if there is a population of students on campus who are consistently exceeding the performance standards on assessments. Meeting only minimum standards would be a cause of concern and these students would need a curricular program that extends their learning and supports their academic growth. In contrast, an effective curricular program would foster academic growth for all students.

15. D: All curriculum and resources should be aligned to standards. Therefore, if standards change, it is likely that the curriculum will need to be revised and new resources purchased. However, before changes in the curriculum can be made, the principal will need to know how the new standards differ from the previous standards. This will help the principal determine if minor revisions to the curriculum are needed or if a new curriculum will need to be adopted.

16. A: Prior to adopting curriculum, the alignment of the curriculum to learning standards must be verified. Curriculum that is not aligned will not be effective in instruction students and ensuring their performance on state-mandated assessments. After the alignment has been verified, the curriculum may be vetted by various stakeholders and approved for use by the school board.

17. B: Instruction can be differentiated based on content, process, or product. Differentiating instruction based on product means that the teacher provides multiple ways for a student to demonstrate mastery. Allowing students to write an essay gives students an opportunity to demonstrate mastery in written form or in spoken form. Providing students with different versions of assessments is still assessing students using a test and does not constitute differentiated instruction.

18. B: To create environments wherein teachers feel safe to express their ideas, school leaders should not criticize even unusual ideas (A); schedule regular, brief times during meetings for teachers to express original ideas (B); abandon their fears that teachers will undermine their authority (C) because leadership experts find that the more a leader shares power, the more authority he or she gains; and ask teachers what elements of a safe environment are similar, not different, for teachers in the school as for students in their classrooms (D).

19. B: To provide teachers with effective feedback and collaboration, school leaders must know that student motivation and learning are influenced by different types of assessments; that despite "objective" tests, machine scoring, etc., ultimately assessment is based in the judgment, assumptions, and values of professional educators who design, score, interpret, and grade assessments; that not only is error inevitable in all assessment, but moreover it is typically underestimated; and that reliability in assessment involves scores and results, *not* tests or instruments.

20. A: The best strategy the principal can use to establish a continuous improvement cycle is to assess students at regular intervals and adjust instruction based on the data. Benchmark exams are typically shorter assessments over selected objectives rather than large comprehensive assessments. Data from these assessments reflect the mastery of objectives that are recently taught and are aligned to the pacing of the curriculum scope and sequence. Testing in less frequent intervals can also be helpful if the data is used to adjust instruction immediately rather than informing plans for the subsequent school year.

21. A: The school leader should make time to collect and analyze student work samples. The audit can be random or the school leader can focus on particular groups of students based on data. However, the school leader should discuss the work samples with the teachers who assigned them. Monitoring grades does not provide the school leader with information about the assignments that were graded. Hosting a science fair and using portfolios for assessment can be beneficial but do not directly indicate that the school leader is involved in these activities.

22. C: Providing teachers with aggregated student data, even in regular intervals, will not likely improve teacher practice. School leaders must disaggregate data to help teachers identify the data that is reflective of their students and their instructional practice. Disaggregated data should also be analyzed in a collaborative process to help identify needs and generate solutions to address those needs.

23. B: Individualized feedback is the most useful observational feedback of the given options. While school leaders should give feedback that is informed by statistics, individualized feedback is more practical and genuinely useful when compared to broad observations. It is ideal that each teacher in a school receive observation and feedback, but quantity and standardization should not be a set goal when it could impact the usefulness of the feedback itself. Each teacher has specific tendencies, strengths, and weaknesses that should be acknowledged to help support their development and effectiveness in reaching educational goals.

24. A: The Supportive School Discipline Initiative (SSDI) included guidance for positive school discipline practices to keep students in school by providing alternatives to exclusionary methods like suspension and expulsion. This guidance was produced jointly by the US Departments of Education and Justice to ensure enforcement of federal civil rights protections against discrimination. It provides school resources with helpful information rather than getting it from them. The SSDI's purpose was to keep student discipline from escalating to the police or prison systems, not to continue this trend.

25. B: The new principal is aware that the teachers on campus are not happy; therefore, it is best to talk to a small group of teachers to understand what issues that they have. Sending a survey out is a good strategy, but not necessarily a first step as the data collected may not thoroughly describe the issues that the teachers have, especially if teachers do not feel that they can be honest on the survey. Also, an all-staff meeting can quickly get out of control if outspoken staff persons have unaddressed issues. Sending an email is impersonal and not an advisable first step.

26. C: The DOJ collaborated with the ED in producing a positive school discipline guidance package as part of the SSDI to prevent or reduce student movement from schools to justice and correctional systems, not match school discipline to practices in those systems; replace disciplinary exclusion with better alternatives, rather than regard student justice involvement as inevitable and wait to address that; ensure Titles IV and VI of the Civil Rights Act prohibiting discrimination are enforced, which is the DOJ's job; and establish fair disciplinary practices to keep all students in school, not exclude any.

27. B: All students are expected to meet the standards outlined by the state and federal government. School leaders are responsible for providing students with the instruction, resources, and support necessary to meet these standards. Equity refers to providing students with the resources and support that meet their individual needs. When leaders implement equity in schools, this may mean that some students receive more resources and support or different resources and support than others. This need may be due to a lack of educational opportunity, physical or intellectual disabilities, or other circumstances. Leaders must be aware of what students need so that the right resources and support can be used to support these students. All students will need resources and support to enrich their education, but practicing equity means that students will receive the appropriate amount of resources based on their identified needs.

28. A: Supporting teachers in conducting action research on campus is an example of giving them opportunities to take risks for improving teaching and learning. Action research allows the teacher to identify the area of improvement and hypothesize which actions or strategies may lead to improving the identified area. Action research allows teachers to problem solve using solutions that they have developed which gives them the opportunity to take risks.

29. D: A school leader should focus on improving all teaching on campus, even teaching that is already considered effective. This reinforces a culture of high expectations on campus and demonstrates to high-performing teachers that they are valued. When a school leader is committed to improving all instruction on campus, even instruction that is considered effective, all staff are encouraged to grow professionally for the benefit of students.

30. C: A successful new teacher induction program will provide opportunities for new teachers to collaborate with one another and with more experienced teachers. Additionally, a successful program will incorporate leadership development opportunities for new teachers to explore and refine their leadership skills. New teachers should receive strategic professional coaching and be assigned a mentor based on experience and effectiveness of the mentoring staff member. While the school leader is responsible for ensuring that an effective induction program in place, there are other instructional staff and campus leaders who can add value to the induction program by facilitating various aspects of the program.

31. D: A physically safe environment is free from dangers, both seen and unseen, that would pose a threat to the physical safety of anyone exposed to the environment. A physically safe environment is in good repair, accessible to all, and accommodating in relation to the nature in which the environment is designated for use.

32. C: According to the Collaborative for Academic, Social, and Emotional Learning (CASEL), effective SEL programs incorporate sequenced and systematic programming across all grade levels, monitor the programming continuously, offer opportunities for students to practice the skills they learn, and coordinate school environments with community environments.

33. B: The action that would best address the challenges in communication, parental engagement, and at home learning is to help the parents learn English by offering ESL classes on campus. Hosting the classes on campus encourages parents to engage with the school community and reinforces that the school values the presence and engagement of the parents. Having a translator on campus and translating documents for parents are important actions to take but are not long-term solutions to the challenge. Students should not be asked to translate school information for their parents.

34. A: School-wide positive behavior support programs typically have three tiers. In tier 1, all students receive universal instructional and behavioral supports and interventions, which are effective for the majority. In tier 2, a minority of students needing more behavior support receive small-group instruction in academic subjects and emotional and social skills. In tier 3, an even smaller minority not responding to tier 2 interventions receives intensive, individualized interventions.

35. B: Researchers found that, among public schools, those with higher performance than others each seemed to have a unique combination of factors contributing to their success. These factors include having a clear and shared focus, having high expectations and standards for students, and high levels of family and community involvement. An effective school leader is a significant factor in high performing schools but is not the only determinant of success. Similarly, alignment of curriculum and instruction and frequent monitoring of teaching and learning are critical success factors but cannot be deemed the most important. Finally, schools need resources for success, but many public schools have demonstrated success with meager funding.

36. B: When teachers are given the power to choose their own professional development opportunities, they are given the opportunity to reflect on their own practice, identify their strengths and weaknesses, and participate in professional development that they believe is relevant. This contributes to building a risk-taking environment because teachers will be able to examine their own beliefs, values, and practices concerning teaching and learning and determine where they would like to improve.

37. C: To encourage teacher leadership, school leaders must create safe environments wherein teachers can take risks and think creatively. School leaders should share authority with teachers to assist them in developing leadership skills and demonstrate responsibility. Increasing a teacher's workload with work that is not directly related to increased responsibilities or to skill refinement is not an example of developing a teacher. Additionally, leaders must differentiate support for teachers based on the current performance, skill, and attitudes.

38. B: Establishing an anti-discrimination policy helps all staff and students to understand the regulations relating to bias and discrimination on campus. Describing what constitutes bias and discrimination makes it easier to identify violations on campus. Additionally, establishing a committee that is focused on cultural awareness and inclusion can help to decrease educational and institutional bias and discriminatory practices. Establishing and enforcing rules has limited efficacy if there is limited understanding of the rationale behind the rules. Having a culturally diverse staff is beneficial, but persons of underrepresented cultures should not be required to teach others about their cultures if they do not choose to. It is beneficial to include opportunities for students to learn about other cultures in the classroom, however this strategy does not help to identify bias and discriminatory practices on campus.

39. C: Meeting with a diverse group of stakeholders from the community will give the new principal a well-rounded perspective of the community. Researching the community online, reviewing student data, and talking with staff are all effective methods of collecting information, but speaking directly with community members is a better source of more insightful information.

40. A: In diverse communities, school leaders often encounter language barriers when attempting to communicate with parents of students or other community members. While it is helpful when a school leader is fluent in more than one language, there are often a variety of languages that are spoken in these communities. There can be translators, including sign language interpreters, or translation machines available at community meetings when appropriate. There are also many businesses that offer translation services for documents and real-time translation for meetings and conferences.

41. C: The school leader should share the commitment to implementing the school vision and goals not only with school personnel (A), (D), but also with community members (B), (C); these participants should not all share common perspectives (A), (B) but rather should represent the diversity of backgrounds and viewpoints in the school and community (C).

42. B: Successful school principals report that daily morning public announcements (A) are best for communicating school vision to students. For staff, a brief, succinct daily e-mail is best for combining and connecting administrative details and useful information with school vision (B), also showing that principals value staff time. Attending community events (C) is best for communicating school vision to stakeholders beyond campus. Effective meetings are two-way interactions (D), best for staff affirmation, collaborative opportunities, and internal highlight sharing. Most one-way communications can be handled through e-mails (B).

43. A: The best way that the school leader can ensure equitable treatment of students and staff is to develop policies and procedures and adhere to them. When there are policies and procedures in place, the school leader can refer to these to determine their course of action when dealing with students and staff. Policies and procedures help leaders proactively ensure that students and staff are treated equitably because they serve as guidelines for behavior and are not subjective. Creating an advisory committee can assist with developing these policies and procedures, but doing so does not shape the behavior of all staff and students. Additionally, while it is advisable that a school leader addresses student and staff complaints swiftly, this is a reactive response and likely occurs after someone has already been treated in an inequitable manner.

44. B: The Council of Chief State School Officers (CCSSO) standards include developing school cultures and instructional programs promoting student learning and staff professional growth (A); assuring safe, effective learning environments through efficient management of school resources, organization, and operations (C); and responding to needs and interests of diverse community members (D), among others. However, they do not include having students monitor their own data (B), which is otherwise an exemplary school leader policy but not part of these standards for respecting individual worth and dignity.

45. A: Differentiated instruction refers to providing customized or tailored instruction to students to meet their diverse learning needs. Previous academic performance, special needs (such as a physical or learning disability), and learning styles are good ways to determine how to differentiate instruction to meet student needs. Other sources of data, such as interests, career goals, and others can be helpful, but are not always relevant.

46. A: Choice A is the only option that does not directly relate to the specific goal in mind. This step calls for teams who would support specific delays. The students in mind are not necessarily delayed, but are thought to be underperforming according to their ability as a result of inadequate challenge. Choice B relates to the goal because it focuses on identifying students who need to be targeted. Choice C focuses on finding teachers who either need to improve their instructional practices or who have exemplary instructional practices. The implication is that the exemplary teachers may be able to share some of their teaching insights with the PLCs and, thereby, help with developing school-wide best practices. Choice D may not be the best practice as external consultation can be expensive and potentially ineffective, but it does directly relate to the goal and is an effective strategy to improve instructional practices.

47. B: To obtain diverse perspectives from the internal and external community, the school leader should include as many types of stakeholders as possible in the process. Students and staff make up the internal community. Parents and other community members make up the external community. It is effective practice to engage stakeholders in a variety of ways; however, in this scenario, a survey distributed to students, parents, staff, and community members would solicit the most diversity of perspectives.

48. A: Classroom management systems, e.g., tiered school-wide positive behavior support systems, make learning environments orderly, enabling students to learn more easily and succeed academically. Rather than only controlling student behavior, they foster and sustain appropriate classroom behavior while also promoting student emotional and social development. They are effective for increasing both prosocial behavior and academic engagement in students. By providing universal supports in the first-tier school-wide, they succeed for 80-85% of students, while individualized intensive interventions are reserved for the remaining 15-20% in the third tier.

49. D: To help students prepare for their futures, high schools should design curricula relevant to students' lives, communities, and cultural milieus. This includes the career and technical education they will need for today's world, which public high schools must offer. School partnerships with colleges and universities best prepare students for higher education, while community-based and project-based learning best prepare students for employment.

50. B: Although there are many factors and influences outside of the school that can lead a young person to commit suicide, the school and its staff can serve as a resource and support for students who experience suicidal thoughts. A school leader should ensure that there are systems in place on campus that allow students to express their needs so that they can be referred for services. This may include having walk-in counseling hours or open-door policies with key staff members.

51. D: If possible, the school leader should communicate directly with the student and their family to learn about the student's academic, social, and emotional needs. Schools and school districts have policies and procedures for supporting students whose first language is not English so that these students can receive the support that they need to be academically successful. It is unlikely feasible to actually have a permanent translator available for all classes as in choice C, so a better first step is to start with a consultation using a translator temporarily while a plan is made.

52. D: It is beneficial to the school community, the community at large, and postsecondary education institutions to align education expectations between secondary school and postsecondary school. The communication between postsecondary institutions and school leaders can help identify the skills necessary to succeed in college, trends in degree programs, and career paths. This type of communication can also lead to the integration of higher education programming on school campuses, such as dual-credit enrollment or training and certification programs.

53. C: Group consensus is an ideal approach for collaborative decisions in that all participants' voices are heard, and every member must provide input and agree with the group decision. However, it is more time-consuming, not more time-efficient, than majority rule or committee decision-making. Majority rule is the method wherein minority voters' commitment can be undermined. Committee decision-making is the method whereby committee members may feel their time and effort were wasted if members of the larger group frequently override committee decisions.

54. D: The least restrictive environment for a student who receives special education services is the same environment as their peers who do not receive these services. Any time a student is removed from the main program of education, their environment is restricted. A students LRE is determined by their Individualized Education Plan and may differ based on their learning needs. However, a student's IEP and academic performance must be reviewed regularly to ensure that the student is in the least restrictive environment possible.

55. C: Researchers have identified a number of transformational school leader practices promoting organizational staff learning, and the most effective transformational leaders best promote organizational learning by modeling ongoing learning in their own practices and affording staff opportunities to learn from peers. Demonstrating their high expectations for both students and teachers is important, but not necessarily central to organizational learning. While researching effective instructional practices and training staff on implementation is also useful, this approach is less aligned with transformational leadership.

56. B: Research finds the relationship between school leadership and student outcomes is indirect rather than direct. Rather than motivating student achievement directly, effective school leadership promotes a school climate conducive to learning. Substantial research has demonstrated that there is a relationship between school leadership and student outcomes, although the relationship is indirect.

57. A: To be effective, research finds tiered behavior management systems applied at the classroom level should be established early in the school year; however, individual programs for disruptive student behaviors may begin at any time as needed. Classroom behavior management systems should be applied across the grades to give students consistent, ongoing input and reinforcement of procedures, rules, and expectations; and throughout the school year without fading to reinforce and support positive behavior.

58. C: Among many others, NASSP recommendations for promoting student mental health (MH) include providing comprehensive staff development\not only to school employees, but also to community service personnel working in the school; training school and community staff working in the school in promoting school-wide positive environments, which is found effective; training school staff in using referral mechanisms to help students access community MH services; and training both school and community staff working in schools in early identification of MH disorders and risks for these.

59. D: Teachers need opportunities to share their beliefs and ideas about teaching and learning with the school leader and with one another. Teachers must believe that they operate in an environment that allows them to be open and honest when examining their own beliefs and practices. Suggestion boxes and surveys are one-way communication tools that do not allow for peer discussion, although anonymity may help teachers feel comfortable giving honest feedback. Providing collaborative meeting time for teachers and meeting with them regularly gives teachers the opportunity to discuss their ideas with one another but also gives them the opportunity to share their ideas with the school leader when they are comfortable.

60. A: Researchers have found that students' academic self-concepts are *not correlated* with their academic achievement, but *are* correlated with later life successes like employment and earnings. Although socioeconomic status (SES) is related to academic self-concept (as well as achievement and retention), it does *not* correlate as strongly with SES as with students' home educational settings. Although smaller school size is found to benefit student participation as well as principal leadership and teacher distributed leadership, *larger* school size correlates positively with student academic self-concept.

Organizational Development

61. B: Research from Stanford University (Grissom, Loeb, and Master, 2013) into effective school leader use of instructional time finds that improvements in student achievement are predicted by time spent on evaluation of teachers and/or curriculum, coaching teachers, and developing the school education program. It is *not* predicted in informal classroom walkthroughs, particularly in high schools. The investigators speculate this may be because school leaders frequently do not incorporate walkthroughs into broader strategies for school improvement.

62. C: Professional learning communities allow staff with shared roles or responsibilities to collaborate in a way that meets the needs of teachers and students. These communities are usually goal-driven and encourage the sharing of ideas and responsibilities. Professional learning communities are used in a variety of ways, but the primary purpose is to facilitate collaboration among educators.

63. D: Leaders can encourage self-direction in improving among faculty and staff by modeling this behavior. Leaders who are transparent about their own areas of improvement will encourage and set an example for employees. Additionally, the school leader should actively engage employees in self-assessment as well as make resources available for doing so. However, a leader should not leave self-improvement up to employees as it will likely not be done. Employees need support, resources, and encouragement to engage in self-directed improvement.

64. D: A coach is a professional who helps a teacher develop the skills necessary to do their job effectively. A coach is a staff member who does not supervise or evaluate the person being coached. This helps to foster a relationship of trust between the coach and the teacher. A coach will identify a teacher's areas of strength and weakness based on a predetermined rubric or set of expectations. Then the coach will provide one-on-one support to the teacher to help improve targeted areas. A coach may provide books and resources, recommend professional development sessions, model effective teaching methods, observe the teacher in practice to provide real-time feedback, assist in the lesson planning process, and guide the teacher in self-reflection and critical analysis processes. A coach provides individualized, targeted support to teachers and helps them to grow, usually in a shorter period of time than other forms of professional development support.

65. A: Rigor in academic instruction refers to curriculum and instruction that is challenging to students. Rigorous instruction challenges students academically, but also intellectually and even personally. Rigorous instruction is often complex and challenges students to think deeply and critically. Rigor does not mean excessively hard or difficult. However, rigor does involve instruction that is stimulating and engaging. Rigorous instruction often requires students to make connections across academic content areas and apply concepts to the real world.

66. C: Grades should reflect student mastery of objectives. The assistant principal needs to know if the reading teacher is assessing students properly to assign grades and if so, determine why measurements of student progress and mastery are not entered into the gradebook in a timely manner.

67. C: The beginning of the school year is a critical time that can impact the success of the entire school year. Therefore, a leader should strive to have 100% of staff in place before school starts. Important trainings and professional development occur prior to the start of the year. A teacher who is hired later will miss these important trainings, which can impact their efficacy in the classroom and their ability to build relationships with the rest of the instructional team.

68. D: School leaders should not assign teachers to write technology standards. Integrating technology does help students meet curriculum standards. School leaders and faculty should require students to master any existing technology standards as cross-curricular and procedural knowledge and skills. Experts advise school leaders and teachers to focus not on learning about technology, but on learning with technology.

69. C: Study questions at the ends of textbook chapters typically help students recall or identify, locate, interpret, and apply information they just read more than reflect. Graphic organizers help students visualize and organize verbal, numerical, and abstract information. Worksheets help students practice what they have just learned. Writing regularly in journals promotes and gives students a method for reflection.

70. C: Prior to the integration of technology into instructional practice, it was difficult for teachers to individualize instruction for students as it relates to content and pace. Technology applications allow teachers to facilitate instruction that meets the students' individual needs and allows students to work at their own pace toward mastery. Heterogenous student grouping can be a beneficial strategy but is not directly related to technology use in the classroom. Similarly, passive and active learning can occur with or without technology integration. Project-based learning can be facilitated with technology, but it is not a requirement.

71. B: Alternative high school principals (Mohr and Dichter, 2001) identified staff developmental stages of honeymoon, conflict, confusion, messy, scary, and mature, in that order, in becoming learning communities. The honeymoon stage is identified as when a sense of community first emerges. The conflict stage is summarized as "the honeymoon is over." The confusion stage is characterized by staff uncertainty over the leader's role. The messy stage involves increased lack of clarity. The scary stage finds staff wondering where accountability and authority are. The mature stage equates to the birth of a learning community.

72. B: When students have satisfactory academic performance in class (reflected through items such as classroom assignments, teacher-created tests, and projects), but fail to meet satisfactory performance on standardized tests, that is an indication that what is taught in the classroom is not aligned with what is tested. This data trend shows that students are performing well based on the curriculum, but the curriculum does not adequately prepare students for what is assessed on the standardized test.

73. A: Research studies have found the most effective implementations of school data use initiatives were most proactive, offering regular and expert system data use training of school leaders, leadership skills advice and coaching, and vigorous promotion. These got significantly better results even comparing districts using similar data systems, showing implementation was more important than the data system. Researchers observed that, although technology is necessary to support data initiatives, it alone is not the answer to school data use. Studies also found teams use data technology systems more quickly and productively than individual teachers.

74. C: Collaboration requires that the school leader engage directly with teachers to maintain an instructional program that delivers standards-based instruction. PLCs are excellent opportunities to listen and provide input during the planning stage for delivering instruction. Auditing classroom materials and analyzing the accuracy of grading are good tools for evaluating the delivery of standards-based instruction but are not collaborative. Administering a survey about new curriculum is not collaborative and does not help to support implementation of current materials.

75. B: Recognizing and celebrating educational success is an effective strategy to develop positive family and community partnerships. A school leader should make an effort to organize events on campus and in the community to develop positive partnerships. Live events facilitate two-way communication, unlike newsletters which are one-way modes of communication. Attending athletic events and soliciting feedback from the community are additional ways to build a relationship with the community, but the most effective strategy for building a positive partnership is to host an event that spotlights positive things related to the school and students.

76. B: According to researchers (Mitchell and Sackney, 1998), both reflection (i.e., considering their own practices) and conversation (i.e., discussing their and colleagues' practices) enable teachers to have awareness of their own and others' practices, evaluate them, and discover possible alternatives. These are cognitive processes. Affirmation of one another as professionals, and invitation into school decision-making both validate all staff members' contributions, acknowledge individual professional competencies, and thereby establish positive working relationships. These are affective processes.

77. D: Effective new teacher induction programs should focus on supporting not only the new teachers, but also the school leaders who guide them. This requires offering professional development not only to new teachers, but equally to their mentors, school leaders, and other site leaders. Effective induction programs use research-based and standards-based assessment instruments to assess and inform new teacher performance. The ultimate goal of teacher induction programs that make teachers more effective is to improve student achievement.

78. D: Researchers have found that, in more effective schools, novice teachers are assigned students with similar average achievement as students assigned to more experienced teachers; in other words, more effective schools and leaders assign classes more equitably to novice teachers than less effective schools do. More effective schools and leaders do not assign lower-achieving or higher-achieving students to novice teachers, nor do they assign them randomly relative to student achievement.

79. D: Reducing the teachers' teaching styles is not a priority if the teacher is effective at achieving standards in the curriculum. Reducing variability in classrooms throughout the school tends to promote efficiency in purchasing, and in producing testing materials, since each department can use the same materials. This also could allow for benchmarking from class to class, which helps with pacing the curriculum throughout the year. Other procedures and policies, such as bathroom policies or electronic device policies can promote safety by making sure each student is accounted for.

80. D: Hiring a coach that can train teachers to use differentiated instruction and evaluate them for efficacy would be the most effective strategy for increasing the uses of differentiated instruction on campus. An instructional coach can provide individual and collective support and can monitor and encourage continuous implementation of the strategy. Praising teachers who implement differentiated instruction creates a positive climate but does not help teachers who do not know how to implement differentiated instruction to do so. Similarly, providing resources and modeling are not sufficient actions to take to increase the use of differentiated instruction if teachers do not know how to implement it or do not see the benefit in implementing the strategy.

81. C: The principal has expressed a desire to engage in activities related to curriculum and instruction; therefore, assisting with lunch duty would not be an option. Analyzing data is a beneficial activity but is only indirectly related to curriculum and instruction. Similarly, tutoring students one time in isolation would not be beneficial use of the principal's time. Instead, the principal should engage in professional learning communities with teachers to discuss the implementation of curriculum and the results.

82. D: For making appropriate instructional decisions, the principal must be able to identify data required to inform them. Disaggregated standardized test data will inform identifying areas of student mastery and need, and state standards will inform designing curriculum and identifying instructional content. Knowing these together will inform identifying the best instructional strategies to increase student ELA achievement.

83. D: Incorporating new and different instructional goals (D) does not necessarily help with providing rigorous and relevant curriculum design. Significant purposes of rigorous, relevant curriculum design include challenging educator thinking about ways students learn (A) and how they evaluate these; incorporating teachers' instructional skills (B); and applying a structure to organize existing instruction and assessment goals (C) but not introducing new and/or different instructional goals.

84. A: The philosophy of differentiating instruction is compatible with standards-based instruction required for accountability as long as educators apply principles of effective curriculum and instruction. For example, differentiation principles include leading students into Vygotsky's Zone of Proximal Development (where students can do more with assistance than they can alone) to optimize learning (A). Natural learning opportunities aid students in the same manner (B). Activating prior student knowledge not only makes new learning relevant to students but also enables them to learn best (C). A sense of community, wherein students feel respected and important, makes learning more effective both socially and academically (D).

85. C: Effective teachers combine standards-based instruction, enabling students to pass accountability exams with differentiated instruction and addressing individual student differences in skills and learning levels, using teaching methods including these: starting every textbook chapter by defining specific skills and concepts for students to master in each curriculum segment (A); allotting comparable small-group times for advanced, struggling, and mixed-level students (B); dividing classroom time among whole-class, small-group, teacher-led, and independent activities (C); and guiding students to connect new material to their prior learning (D).

86. A: School leaders are responsible for deciding how often and to whom teachers submit data; for example, they might want teachers to submit data every 2 to 3 weeks to their team leaders to enable structured data discussions during team meetings. School leaders are responsible to ensure teachers collect data continuously: quarterly (B) is insufficient to adjust instruction, can impede viewing monitoring as essential, and fails to further faculty instruction and assessment goals. School leaders are also responsible for helping faculty choose and develop data-recording forms (C) and ensuring faculty application of state-assigned rubrics to predict student performance on state assessments (D).

87. D: School leaders must collaborate with faculty and other staff to design curriculum and instruction (A); review programs regularly not only to determine correct implementation (B) but also to identify students' unmet educational needs despite implementing programs accurately (C); and in the event of such unmet needs, help faculty and other staff identify content and practices that will address these (D).

88. B: The practice recommended by education authorities is for principals to collaborate with not only curriculum specialists and school professionals (A), for example, faculty, educational specialists, therapists, and so on; not only students and professionals (C); and not only professionals and board of education members (D) but curriculum specialists, professionals, and members of the board of education in making curriculum decisions.

89. D: School leaders must know how to help teachers learn new instructional methods, and how to predict how long it will take for them to learn these (A); how much time effective planning takes, which varies with the number of students to be taught (B); how to network teachers learning new approaches as the school leaders implement these approaches (C); and how much time effective planning will take, which also varies with the levels at which teachers will instruct students in academic content (D).

90. B: School leaders who form data inquiry teams of teachers should not be the ones who directly develop action plans, but should direct these teams to develop action plans based on their analyses of student assessment data. They should assign the teams to implement these plans; supporting their implementation (B) is the school leader's job. School leaders should also rely on their teams to analyze data from both formative and summative assessments (C) by classes, student subgroups, and individual students (D).

91. A: The components of an effective plan include action steps, persons responsible, time frames, milestones, resources needed, and evidence of implementation. The plan will include the resources needed to accomplish the plan so that these resources are planned for and obtained, thus preventing delay in the plan's accomplishment. The evidence of implementation should be included in the plan so that ongoing monitoring can take place. Depending on the aspect of the plan, evidence of implementation could include documents, visible indicators, or regular meetings.

92. A: The first step that a principal should take is to collect information about the resources and strategies currently in place. This will help the principal identify what aspects of the instructional program to keep, adjust, or eliminate. Budgeting and other instructional decisions should not be made until it is determined what the cause of the deficiencies in math are. Additional testing is not necessary because the principal has sufficient data to determine that there is a deficit in math.

93. D: The most appropriate response that the principal can offer the PTO president is that the science curriculum purchase directly supports a school goal. All school resources such as curriculum should be aligned to the school vision and goals. Satisfactory student performance is not an appropriate response given that the school leader may have identified college preparation as an area of improvement, even if students were already meeting expectations in this area. Additionally, the cost of the curriculum is irrelevant if the curriculum is not aligned to the campus vision and goals.

94. C: To address weak areas, it is better to implement strategies that are backed by research and have been proven to yield good results. This can save the campus the time, effort, and resources that would be wasted if untested and unproven strategies were implemented unsuccessfully. When a leader is looking for strategies to foster change on campus, using research-based and proven best practices is beneficial because there will be a clear direction as to how to successfully implement the strategy and a realistic idea of what results to expect. When untested strategies are implemented, the outcome is less certain. Untested strategies also often take more research and a process of trial and error, or a learning curve, to implement, both of which can delay the implementation of change.

95. B: The goal is for both teachers and students to improve their computer skills; providing training to teachers or a new course for students does not fully address the school goal. Purchasing updated computers for students and teachers and training them to use the devices best demonstrates that the leader is using school resources to support the school goal.

96. B: All of the data mentioned would be useful for the school leader to analyze; however, data related to student performance, student attendance data, and student promotion rates are the most comprehensive and informative for the development or revision of the school vision and goals. This data can assist in developing goals that are aligned with federal and state accountability requirements. Analyzing data related to teaching staff and the community are important for understanding and improving campus culture and supporting the instructional goals, but are not the most beneficial when compared to student data. Similarly, school accountability ratings can be helpful to analyze but do not provide sufficient information related to current practice and to the areas of deficit that need to be addressed in the school goals.

97. A: The next step after developing the school vision and goals is to develop a plan for implementing them. The plan should be developed prior to presenting the vision and goals to staff and other stakeholders so that, when they are presented, these stakeholders can be informed of their roles and responsibilities related to implementation of the vision and goals. It is important for a school leader to delegate tasks to other leaders on campus in relation to the vision and goals, but the plan must be developed first for the leader to know which tasks to delegate.

98. A: A leader effectively monitors goal progress by implementing clear checkpoints and milestones for goal activities. Each goal should be broken down into smaller goals, or milestones, that can be reviewed at regular intervals. This allows the leader to analyze progress toward the goal on a timeline so that if there is not sufficient progress toward the goal, there is time to intervene and make changes to the action steps.

99. D: School leaders should use both quantitative and qualitative data to inform the school vision, mission, and goals. Assessment data and grades are important data points, but of the options provided, combining data from assessments and from stakeholder feedback would provide the most comprehensive data. Formative assessment may include course grades, benchmark exams, and other data points. Summative assessments may include standardized tests or campus-based exams for credit or matriculation.

100. B: Hosting a community meeting to communicate the school vision pertains to the implementation stages of vision and goals, not the development and planning stage. To create a shared vision, the school leader should make the vision relevant to the community, solicit community input, and based the vision and goals on data. After the vision has been developed with the community in mind, the vision can be shared with others.

101. B: Change is often opposed when stakeholders feel that the change is done without their consent and is outside of their control. As a result, obtaining stakeholder buy in can help make changes more effective. Goals should align to the changes but this strategy by itself will not help to manage the change. Additional training will be ineffective if stakeholders are opposed to the change. School leaders should listen to those who are opposed to the change and attempt to address their concerns rather than removing them from campus.

102. C: School leaders must ensure in advance that most that the specific responsibilities of each member of the command and control group are clearly defined for a variety of different crisis situations. Tenure is not an equitable way of selecting members. Distributing leadership could cause confusion during a crisis, and a complex reporting system could defeat the whole purpose of such a team.

103. A: Vision and goals are deemed appropriate when they are based on multiple sources of data that reflect current practice. It is important for school leaders to solicit buy in from community members, but this is not an indicator of the appropriateness of the goals. Additionally, the school vision and goals can leverage school strengths, but areas of deficit or weakness are often addressed in the goals. Although schools may have similar demographics and performance history, the school vision and goals should be based upon a thorough analysis of the data unique to the campus. Consequently, the vision and goals of schools may differ even though the performance history and demographics of the school may appear to be similar.

104. C: Buy in from internal and external community members would be the most likely strategy for engaging stakeholders in the implementation of the school vision and goals. Buy in is achieved when stakeholders are included in the process of developing the school vision and goals. When stakeholders are part of the process, they are more likely to feel ownership of the product which motivates them to engage in implementation. Communicating the school vision and goals to the community is important, but it may not lead to engagement in implementation if stakeholders do not feel that they were including in the process of developing the vision and goals.

105. A: The process of continuous improvement is the ongoing act of assessing performance and adjusting efforts in order to improve that performance. In order to implement a process of continuous improvement, there must be procedures of evaluation developed and implemented at regular checkpoints. Based on these regular evaluations, the leadership team can identify areas of improvement and initiate interventions and actions based on those identified areas. In schools, the regular evaluation of progress toward the campus vision and goals can be developed into a process of continuous improvement. However, campus leaders must focus on both the strengths and weaknesses of the campus in this process. Deficient areas can be improved to perform to standard, while areas performing at standard can be innovated for improvement.

106. D: All the choices are benefits of gathering the data, but the primary benefit is obtaining multiple sources of data to accurately identify the strengths, needs, gaps, and areas of improvement for the school. The school leader chose a combination of quantitative and qualitative data to accurately assess school performance and the cultures, values, attitudes, and beliefs that impact that performance. It is important to use data from multiple sources to develop the school vision and goals because using only one source of data may portray a limited or skewed picture of the school. Using multiple sources of data can confirm the validity of data and provide a more complete picture of the complex dynamics of a school campus.

107. A: Leaders intent on fostering change are required to strategically communicate the intended change and gather supporters for that change. First, the leader needs to communicate the intended change effectively. Many people are unwilling to support changes because they fear the unknown. The leader should communicate not only what is to be changed but also how the changes affect the various staff members and how the changes are aligned to the school vision and goals.

108. D: Of the choices presented, choice D is the most valid. Leaders should seek to share substantial academic gains with the community with regularity to try to capture the attention and support of families and entities, such as businesses, in the community. The other options are not very generalizable or necessarily relevant to school goals in general, so they are not as applicable to the scenario.

109. A: Before engaging any community resource, school leaders must consider whether it is compatible with the school's vision and mission. Some resources may have impact in the long-term rather than immediately and should not be discarded because effects will not be seen immediately. Additionally, as communities develop, new resources may be made available. Not all available resources will have a history of prior implementation but may prove beneficial for student learning. Similarly, as the school builds new partnerships, community resources may become available through new community relationships.

110. D: Behavioral codes of conduct govern student, faculty, staff, and visitor behavior in schools. State regulations typically require schools to give teachers copies upon adoption, send all parents summaries before school years start, and give students copies when school years begin. However, to gain stakeholder buy in and to assure collective understanding and agreement, conduct codes can be developed jointly by parents, teachers, and students.

111. A: Research shows that, among others, one reason schools should collaborate with their communities to provide mental health services is that schools are not suitable settings for clinical psychiatric care and similar services. When collaborating with communities, school staff must work not only with families and community service providers, but also with policymakers to coordinate and connect needed support processes. A cohesive and integrated mental health intervention continuum must address both severe student problems and universal student needs.

112. D: Schools and communities benefit mutually from school leader outreach. For example, community partners become better informed about school functions and needs and develop a sense of ownership in the school. They appreciate and remember the invitations, acknowledgements, and thanks of school leaders. School leaders show they recognize their school belongs to the community by offering community access to school facilities for various events, benefiting not only the community but also the school when community members gain better understandings of the school and its positive effects on student lives.

113. D: Community outreach, encouraging family volunteers, and serving on PTAs is predominantly the responsibility of school leaders, rather than the collective responsibility of school leaders. Supporting parenting skills(A), actively participating in and encouraging parents to participate in student learning, and engaging parents to become partners for school decision making are collaborative efforts, as the teachers, faculty, and staff are likely to have much more direct contact with the parents than a school leader is capable of maintaining. These processes help to build a school community and are supported throughout the community, not only by the leadership.

114. B: In many American states and communities, schools are usually the primary mental health (MH) service providers for children. Schools have an obligation to provide services for students if those services pertain to the access and availability to education. When services like clinical psychiatric care are often infeasible and inappropriate in schools (B), school and community MH services often must be integrated within the care continuum provided by schools. IDEA law provides that all public schools must provide access to services that facilitate a Free and Appropriate Public Education (FAPE), including mental health services. In the case that a school is unable to provide a needed service to a student, the school may collaborate with external resources to ensure the student receives all of the provisions they require. This is a common practice in many school districts when services are infeasible or inappropriate. Choices A and C imply that a school needs to provide students and parents not only with necessary services, but with a broad choice of providers and environment, which is not true. A school must only provide sufficient services, not necessarily a choice of providers and locations. School-based services are services provided through the school district, but they do not preclude students and parents from seeking private help if they desire a specific service provider or location for services. Choice D implies that students would prefer external resources, but it does not imply that the resources provided are ineffective or insufficient for the needs of students. If, however, students are seeking external services that should be provided, the school should look into adding these as options.

115. B: School leaders and other educators should involve families in collaborative educational design as they are their children's primary advocates (A). Families can advocate for other families within school-based dialogues (C), and they can offer service and support to schools in developing learning communities (D). However, when family participation is limited to an elite minority who volunteer, other families are more likely to feel intimidated against participating than inspired to participate (B).

116. D: Researchers find that public engagement in education strengthens local safety and security (A), improves public perceptions of school reform efforts (B), revitalizes communities as well as helping schools (C), and increases the participation of citizens and students in both school service and community service (D).

117. A: Measures of how school community engagement strategies affect students include their greater academic achievement and fewer school behavior problems (A); increased school attendance and increased school enrollment (B); higher school enrollment and achievement (C); and increased satisfaction along with achievement (D).

118. A: Effective school leaders must clarify what they need, what stakeholders want, and how these can coincide to communicate and determine partnership feasibility. They must adjust language for businesspeople. For example, business executives use more proactive than reactive language (B). School leaders should determine whether their visions and/or missions match other's, but these need not match exactly (C). They can overlap, and school leaders must identify these overlaps. Though a few rare businesspeople are altruistically motivated by school benefits, most must hear what they will get from partnership (D).

119. C: Depending on school budget and resources, student needs that are not directly related to student safety and academic performance may not be able to be addressed using school resources. Many community resources used to support schools are targeted toward students in need. These types of resources may address physical needs of students and their families, such as providing food, clothing, toiletries, haircuts and grooming, or helping adults find jobs.

120. D: Letters and automated calls are acceptable forms of communication, but communication is most effective when parents and community members have the opportunity to engage in two-way conversation. Hosting a meeting gives participants a chance to ask questions and provide feedback to school leadership.

Systems Leadership

121. D: Because research studies repeatedly prove student benefits of smaller class sizes, school leaders must hire and retain adequate human resources in terms of quantity and quality. For a safe, comfortable teaching and learning environment, school leaders must provide adequate physical resources like space, furniture, lighting, temperature control, etc. They must manage fiscal resources well to manage all other resources, not just some.

122. A: According to the American Association of School Administrators (AASA) Center for System Leadership, applying systems thinking to school reform results in, among other things, continuous improvement of school system policies and practices. Curriculum is aligned system-wide, not diversified. The school system grows in interconnection with other community systems and does not become independent. Priorities are identified and resources are allocated accordingly for universal student success, not only targeted student groups.

123. C: Narrative writing tells a story. School leaders need narrative writing skills to relate school success stories. They need persuasive writing skills to convince others to agree with the positions they take, opinions they express, and actions they propose. They might use descriptive writing skills to paint vivid pictures for readers of school activities and situations. They need expository writing skills for informing their readers of facts, statistics, plans, procedures, and other objective information.

124. B: In recent decades, environmental quality issues have emerged that affect school facility operations management. These include asbestos, radon, and other hazardous materials control; energy conservation; and improvement of water, indoor air quality, and acoustics, which may all involve district support in hiring expert facility consultants. Since school leaders have government guidelines with school policies and procedures already in place for food services (A); transportation (C) and custodial (D) services that have existed longer than environmental awareness, they are less likely to require expert consultation.

125. C: An integrated management system unites all digital management systems into one total structure, facilitating shared objectives and working as a unit to achieve them. According to experts, a school not using any digital management system is not the best candidate without experience or systems to integrate. A school using one system and not planning more does not need integration.

The ideal school uses one or more systems and plans adding more. Systems within an integrated management system share policies, documentation, processes, and procedures; a school wanting these separated does not want integration.

126. A: According to the National Education Association (NEA), a school acceptable use policy (AUP) should include a preamble explaining need for an AUP; its goals and development; a school conduct code inclusion of online activity; a definition section of important terms; a policy statement of computer services covered and conditions required for student use (e.g., taking a computer responsibility class); an acceptable uses section *and* unacceptable uses section; and a violations and sanctions section, which should tell students how to report policy violations or question policy application (which may conform to the school disciplinary code), not just define violations.

127. A: The number of math and reading teachers and the size of their classes most directly impact student learning. Research has demonstrated that class size is an influencing factor of student performance and that reducing class sizes to assist struggling students is effective. School start time, testing intervals, and access to technology indirectly impact student learning.

128. A: According to the US Department of Education's Privacy Technical Assistance Center (PTAC) and the National Institute of Standards and Technology (NIST), a school data breach response *policy* defines staff roles and responsibilities; metrics and standards; and reporting, remediation, and feedback mechanisms. Identifying necessary management support and school resources is a function of the data breach response *plan*. Standardizing response tasks and behaviors and preventing errors from being introduced are functions of *procedures* developed based on the plan. Regular risk assessments are a function not of these components but a recommended broader information management strategy.

129. A: The logistics function of the ICS identifies services and resources for supporting incident response needs. The planning function collects and evaluates information, identifies incident response issues, develops action plans, and recommends future actions. The command function manages incidents overall and is directly responsible for public safety, information, and community response agency liaisons. The operations function develops objectives, organizes resources, and directs actions and resources for incident responses.

130. C: Developing a school safety plan requires participation by the entire community because schools with the most numerous and severe violence and crime incidents are in communities with the same characteristics. School leaders and staff are not the only ones (A) because addressing community issues reflected in schools requires collaboration among resources contributing varied expertise and because schools are for learning, not controlling (B) violence or crime. Not only law enforcement and mental health personnel (D) but also parents, community leaders, business leaders, and other community professionals serving youth should participate as well as students, teachers, and administrators.

131. C: Allowing for variations across states, most public-school districts receive the largest proportion of funding from their state governments. According to the American Association of School Administrators (AASA), the federal government provides between 10 and 20 percent of the funding public school districts receive. Local and intermediate governments combined contributing slightly less than the state government. Only a very small proportion of funding comes from other sources.

132. B: In most public school districts, typically the District Office of Achievement and Accountability makes preliminary enrollment projections to inform school budgets. They do not do this alone because of the difficulty of projecting. Instead, they submit their projections to school leaders, who revise them as needed. School leaders do not project their schools' enrollment alone. Final enrollment projections are made by district committees representing not only the Finance and Student Support offices, but also district Achievement and Accountability and Operations offices.

133. D: The term decentralization refers to the transfer of power and authority from the school districts to principals to make decisions related to budgets and staffing. In centralized school districts, the central office determines campus spending and the principal has little to no control over how funds are used. In decentralized school districts, principals have greater control over how to use the funds allotted to their school campus.

134. C: Student growth is the best data point to inform the principal as to whether the math intervention program was effective and should continue to be funded. Student growth can be calculated by comparing student performance in math at the beginning of the school year to the end of the school year. Although standardized test performance is an important data point, this data alone will not indicate the efficacy of the program, especially for students who may have grown significantly, but not enough to meet standardized test performance requirements.

135. B: The principal should consider the campus vision and goals when determining how to allocate resources, including technology resources. The first step that a principal should take when considering spending school funds is determining how the purchase will support the achievement of the vision and goals. When considering upgrading or replacing technology, it is appropriate for the principal to evaluate the current condition of the technology or seek ways to save money; however, the first step that should be taken is to determine if the spending is in alignment with the school goals and vision.

136. D: An effective school leader is transparent when making decisions. This transparency includes sharing data and/or rationale for making decisions. The school leader has already determined that the fine arts program should be discontinued so the best action for the principal to take next is to explain the rationale for that decision to the school community.

137. A: School leaders must abide by policies set forth by local safety departments. In this case, a fire drill may be disruptive to the school day, but it is a priority and must be conducted. In the future, the principal should plan when to conduct fire drills in advance rather than waiting and possibly failing to conduct them.

138. C: It is most important for the school leader to identify the appropriate staff to manage the physical plant. This staff member has the primary responsibility to ensure the safe functioning of everything on campus; therefore, the leader must choose the right staff member for the job and monitor the performance of that staff member. While it is important for the school leader to personally inspect their campus on a regular basis, management of the physical plant must be delegated to an appropriate staff member to ensure that the campus is maintained appropriately.

139. A: Budget planning and operations coordination are two aspects of using technology to support effective school organization management. Notifying stakeholders of meetings is an aspect of using technology to facilitate effective and timely communication. Collecting, disaggregating, and analyzing different school data is an aspect of using technology to manage information. Facilitating multiple stakeholder contributions to projects is an aspect of using technology to enhance collaboration.

140. C: Creating a grief counseling group in response to the death of a student is a positive action, but is reactive, not proactive. An education leader cannot predict every occurrence that may impact student mental and emotional health, but the education leader can create processes and structures that can support students ongoing emotional safety. These can include designing referral systems for mental health care, providing information about available resources to students and their parents, and using school resources to provide mental health support.

141. B: While staying informed of new trends and technology is useful in this role, it is not central to the actual implementation of a new technology that is in its early implementation. Change management often requires more direct support of a wide range of needs from staff and students. Demonstrating the use of the technology (choice A), setting expectations and encouraging effort (choice C), and helping with implementation (choice D) all are a more direct way the school leader should help to implement change in this situation. Both question and answer are highlighted.

142. D: According to some school consensus-building models, although the ideal is for 100% of faculty members to agree to implement a recommendation, this is not always realistic and is not required 100% of the time. If consensus seems impossible, many schools have a rule stating that 80% of members agreeing is sufficient; dissenting members must promise not only to refrain from obstructing implementation, but furthermore to support it.

143. B: Campus-based personnel are dedicated to the campus and work under the direct supervision of the campus principal. District personnel are supervised by other district personnel but provide services to campuses. In many public schools, transportation workers, food service workers, and psychologists are district personnel who provide services to more than one campus. However, in general, most school counselors are dedicated to one campus and are supervised by the school principal.

144. B: Effective induction programs offered by the New Teacher Center and others have impacts on schools of making new teachers more effective, increasing teacher retention rates, strengthening teacher leadership, addressing education inequities, *and* increasing student learning and achievement.

145. A: A school leader should evaluate technology data systems used in the school by how well they provide relevant data for decision making. Affordability and whether other schools are using the data system are important questions to ask when considering purchasing a data system but are less relevant when evaluating the system after use. User friendliness is not as important in evaluation if training and support are readily available to staff who will use the data system.

146. B: School leaders and district personnel can usually project employee salaries for the next school year fairly easily, but it is more difficult to predict healthcare or other employee benefits. Although transportation expenses are essential, they are *not* included in school budgets. Not only are regular school buses and drivers expensive, individual transportation plans included in special education students' Individualized Education Program (IEPs) are even more so, and furnishing homeless and/or other students with transportation is yet another expense. In addition, school district planners *must* reserve some amount of the budget for unexpected emergency school facility repairs, etc.

147. A: Experts have identified four purposes of school technology use: productivity, information access, cognitive stimulus, and instruction content. Databases, word processing programs, spreadsheet programs, and other application software can all be classified as productivity tools. Applying these tools to problem solving and information management is an example of using technology as a productivity tool. Using technology as information involves the Internet and associated information technologies; as a cognitive stimulus involves giving students real-life experiences and authentic simulations to extend learning and stimulate cognitive development; and as instructional content by employing advanced digital content for teaching, drilling, and practicing.

148. C: Although the fundamental American right to information access is important, it is not the only or most important factor in school acceptable use policies (AUPs). Some school districts require student agreement and parental permission forms for minor (under 18) students for independent electronic information use, but this is not always the case. Student intellectual freedom depends on their responsibility for accepting limits in that freedom. Experts do advise schools to contact electronic freedom of information organizations to inform themselves fully.

149. B: Hazard analysis: analyzing food service operation and determining likely food safety hazards and control measures. Identifying CCPs: identifying those few control measures absolutely essential to food safety. Determining critical limits: cooking temperatures, times, and other observable and measurable safety-defining boundaries. Establishing CCP monitoring procedures: tracking CCP control as food flows through operations. Planning corrective actions: planning what to do when a critical limit at a CCP is not met and communicating to and training employees in preventive decisions. Verification procedures: ensuring a scientifically sound system for effective hazard control. Record-keeping system: documenting the HACCP system and plan.

150. B: School leaders are directly responsible for allocating budget for school maintenance and inspections. They should assign experienced maintenance supervisors to develop specific inspection and maintenance procedures (A) and schedules (C) and should oversee the implementation of preventive maintenance procedures, which they cannot directly implement by themselves (D).

151. A: The National Education Association (NEA) identifies essential components of any school Acceptable Use Policy (AUP), including a preamble and definition section; an acceptable uses section (B), defining appropriate student internet use; an unacceptable uses section (C), defining prohibited uses, behaviors, and Web sites; a policy statement (D) identifying covered services and student use conditions; and a violation and sanctions section (A) informing students how to question policy applications and report violations, which may conform to the general school disciplinary code.

152. D: One benefit of having a centralized budget is that tracking and planning expenses tend to be more efficient since the locus of control is not as distributed among a plurality of leaders. In a decentralized budget, each school plans its own budget, at least in part. In this system, there is more potential for the mismanagement of funds, since the budgetary and purchasing decisions are given to more people. Decentralized budgets do have the benefit of flexibility in purchasing and potential for buy in from staff members and leaders, since it allows for decisions to come from people who are closer to campus needs. In the case of a centralized budget, leadership should make particular effort to become aware of individual campus needs. In the case of a decentralized budget, it is important to make sure there are effective means of financial accountability in place. Answer C is not a factor that would be directly affected by budgets being centralized or decentralized.

153. A: Goals for school leaders related to their school safety plans include leading school needs assessments, safety plan development, and implementation monitoring; developing a system to track, report, and give feedback on school incidents and crime and communicating this information to stakeholders (B); designing safe traffic patterns to, from, and within the school rather than appointing others to do this (C); and not only adopting emergency evacuation procedures but also adopting crisis management procedures for the school rather than delegating this (D).

154. A: Conducting drills prepares school staff for responding in a timely, organized, efficient manner in the event of an actual emergency. Drills do not prevent (B) emergencies but prepare people for them. Though response (C) is prominently featured in the question description as the focus of drills, staff are not actually responding during drills but preparing to respond if or when the need should arise. Recovery (D) follows response; neither occurs without an actual emergency.

155. C: It is critical for the school leader to communicate progress toward the school vision and goals to the school community and other stakeholders within the community. The vision and goals outline the direction and focus of the school and all other activities must align to the vision and goals. Activities such as volunteering, mentoring, and collaborating should be in alignment with the school vision and goals; therefore, it is most important for stakeholders to be informed of the school vision and goals and how the school is making progress in these areas.

156. B: Schools and school leaders use data they have collected for setting goals aligned with their school vision and mission. Data-based decision-making is a best practice for school leaders. Data should be collected for all decision making and data can be collected in the forms of quantitative data, such as standardized assessment results, attendance rates, etc., or qualitative data such as survey feedback. School goals must be aligned with the school vision and mission so that progress toward established goals is connected to achieving the school vision and mission.

157. C: When developing a vision and goals for the school, the school leader must ensure that the vision and goals align with the local, state, and federal policies. Local, state, and federal policies include curriculum and assessment standards that must be adhered to. The school leader must determine whether the focus on a fine arts program would assist the school in meeting these standards. If not, it would not be appropriate to include the fine arts program in the school vision and goals. The number of students currently participating in the program is not relevant to the determination. Additionally, the assessment of human and fiscal resources occurs after the vision and goals have been developed.

158. A: Data showing school improvement goals that are behind schedule indicate a need to update the school improvement plan—either by adjusting completion time criteria if school leaders and staff determine they were unrealistic in either case, or by adjusting instruction to be more effective if they determine current methods are delaying progress.

159. B: Ways that school leaders have appropriately involved students in school improvement efforts include allowing students to plan school-wide forums (A), conduct school-wide surveys (B), participate in hiring school leaders (C), and testify before education committees in their state legislatures, which is legal (D).

160. C: All of these questions are important to consider when developing school goals. However, aligning the school goals to the school vision is most critical. The school vision describes how the school is envisioned to be in the future and the school goals are the steps that will enable the school to accomplish that vision.

161. D: Measurable goals can be quantified, and non-measurable goals cannot be quantified. This goal is measurable because calculating the percentage of students who earned at least a B average in their math class can reveal whether or not the goal was met. It also identifies how students are expected to perform in order to reach the goal. When goals are measurable, it is easy to determine whether or not the goal has been met.

162. C: School leaders and others should analyze school data based upon formative classroom assessments and standardized state summative assessments. The data analyzed should include data across grade levels, across school years, by subjects, by student cohorts, by student special populations, and by individual teachers, when possible. Analysis of data should be holistic in order to identify school strengths, needs for improvement, and trends to properly inform the school vision and mission.

163. D: When school visions are developed through collaboration among employees, they tend to be more appropriate to the contexts of their local school districts, which is an advantage. Collaboratively developed school visions typically are *not* implemented as quickly as those personally developed by school leaders, which also tend to be clearer and more coherent than those developed collaboratively. Collaboratively developed school visions do take longer to develop, slowing change, which is a disadvantage, not an advantage.

164. A: Research studies find that, for implementing school-wide technology adoption, required factors are sufficient resources and support, professional development, school structure, school organization, and leadership. Effective professional development must be intentionally and carefully planned, designed with goals in mind, provided continually to keep up with constant changes in the teaching profession, and integrated system-wide or school-wide as part of the school culture through teacher collaboration and sharing of knowledge.

165. C: In school change processes, first-order changes represent specific strategies for implementing deeper changes in educational ideas and philosophies. Thus, forming a different instructional approach is a second-order change, as are forming new interactions and relationships and forming a sense of collaborative ownership among educational stakeholders. For implementing that sense of shared ownership, forming site-based school advisory councils is an example of a corresponding first-order change.

166. Essay question graders commonly look for the following elements in a strong response: strong content knowledge, clear organization, and effective arguments or examples. Language and usage are not usually strictly graded, but they can make a big impact on the clarity of your ideas.

Please use the provided rubric to make sure your response meets these common criteria. Try to have a friend or family member grade your response for you or take a break after writing your response and return to grade it with fresh eyes.

Constructed Response Rubric

Domain	Description
Content Knowledge	• The response directly addresses every part of the prompt. • The response demonstrates independent knowledge of the topic. • The response discusses the topic at an appropriate depth.
Organization	• The response introduces the topic, usually with a thesis statement or by restating the prompt. • The response directly addresses the prompt by providing a clear and concise answer or solution. • The answer or solution is supported by logical arguments or evidence. • The response restates the main idea in the conclusion.
Arguments and Examples	• The response provides a reasonable answer to the prompt. • The answer is supported by strong reasoning or evidence. • The response develops ideas logically and connects ideas to one another. • The reasoning and evidence provided act to support a unified main idea.
Language and Usage	• The response demonstrates effective use of grammar and uses varied sentence structure throughout the response. • The response demonstrates correct use of spelling, punctuation, and capitalization. • The response demonstrates strong and varied use of vocabulary relevant to the topic and appropriate for the intended audience.